DOCTOR GEORGE

AND OTHER SHORT STORIES

NEIL BUTTER

Doctor George and Other Short Stories

Copyright © 2007 Neil Butter

ISBN: 978-1-84799-897-2

All rights reserved. No part of this publication may be reproduced, stored in a retrieval system, or transmitted in any form or by means, electronic, mechanical, photocopying, recording, or otherwise, without the prior permission of the publishers.

Dedication

This collection of short stories, spoofs and vignettes is dedicated to all those who find pleasure in life`s absurdities. But a word of caution: some of the stories are suitable only for laid-back readers, and a few are quite simply unsuitable.

Contents

DOCTOR GEORGE 1
PUPPY LOVE 7
COUNTRY AIR... 13
A QUIET DAY.. 15
WHERE`S THE BODY? 21
PARLOUR GAMES 27
HARD TIMES 31
CECIL AND THE TENTH COMMANDMENT......................... 35
WHAMBO... 43
NAKED AMBITION 45
HELP YOURSELF 49
CLUBBING 53
THE CHRISTMAS SPIRIT 55
SAVANNAH HEAT 61
MUSICAL CHAIRS 67
AND NOW THE FUTURE... 69
A NIGHT AT THE OPERA 73
PRIVATE LIVES.. 79
A CERTAIN AGE 81
A FLIGHT OF FANCY 87
HOLIDAY OF A LIFETIME 91
BRASS NECK 97
LESSONS... 99
KEEPING WATCH 103
THE BARE TRUTH.. 107
THE POOL... 109
CLASS WARFARE 115
CHILD`S PLAY 119
ROOM SERVICE 121
THE FACTS OF LIFE... 123
QUESTION TIME IN THE HOUSE OF COMMONS 125
CHRISTMAS NEWSLETTER.. 129
TAKING THE OATH... 135

DOCTOR GEORGE

No one ever calls me by my surname. People just call me "George" or sometimes "Doctor George". That's because I am a doctor of philosophy. My degree had nothing to do with philosophy, but I like using the letters "Ph.D." They sound impressive. Also it's a bit of a joke when I pay my fortnightly visit to the mental home where my old mother is detained.

"Good morning, Doctor George," the woman receptionist-cum-nurse-cum-warder says when I arrive. "A professional visit to your mother?"

The same thing happened today. Then, as I walked along the Victorian corridor that smelt of lino and polish and disinfectant, I was accosted by an old crow. She was wearing a dressing-gown that looked like a battle-dress.

"Are you a doctor?" she asked.

"Well, yes and no," I replied.

"Either you are or you aren't," she snapped. She might be a patient here, but she had her wits.

"I have a doctorate but not in medicine, so I suspect that I'm not what you want."

She studied me suspiciously. "Bastard!" she spat after a few moments' thought.

Since I couldn't think of a suitable reply, I continued along the corridor until I came to the communal room at the end. My mother would, I knew, be sitting there in her usual arm-chair by one of the windows. (Other patients who had tried to occupy that position had soon discovered her ability to lash out.)

"Hi, mother!"

She looked at me carefully and, after a pause, smiled feebly. "Hallo, Josie, come to see your old Mum, have you?"

"It's George actually. But how are you today?"

She was looking old and thin and weak. Although it was a warm day, she kept her favourite blanket wound round her.

"I know my daughter when I see her so it's no use you pretending that you are George. He was carried off years ago if I remember rightly. Not that I can remember much but I can remember that. Nice boy he was too, I do remember that."

A man who appeared to be in his late eighties tottered over to us. "Would you like to see my dick?" he inquired pleasantly of me.

"Charles! That's no way to speak to my daughter. Be off with you, you old swine."

The man bowed. "I'm sorry, your Grace. No offence meant." He wandered off.

My mother looked at me apologetically. "He's not bad most of the time but he gets a bit funny when there's a full moon. Is there a full moon?"

"No, I think there's only a half-moon at the moment."

"That's odd. I hope he's not going to be a nuisance every day of the month. I shall leave this place altogether if he is. There's nothing wrong with me, you know, except that I am getting a bit ancient."

"So you haven't had any more of your turns?"

"What do you mean *turns* ? Are you suggesting I am going mad?"

"Certainly not! I was just, well, wondering if you had had any more messages from Joan of Arc?"

My mother looked away, then back at me, her face suddenly contorted with rage. "What if I have? What business is it of yours? Why are you always interfering, you slut?"

At that moment, a young psychiatric nurse came into the room wearing a pony tail and a white coat. His deferential manner bordered on the obsequious. His smile was so thin it was almost anorexic.

He had obviously heard the last part of the conversation. It confirmed my suspicions. The room was bugged.

"Now, don't upset yourself," he said to my mother. "I want to take er…. Doctor George away for a quiet word. Come along with me."

My mother sat glowering in her chair. I followed the nurse out of the room into a nearby office. A middle-aged woman, seated behind a large desk, introduced herself. "Hallo, I'm the doctor in charge." She had grey tightly-tied hair, wire-framed spectacles and a serious expression. I hated her on sight.

She looked up from some notes. "Josie, there are a few things we need to discuss."

"I am George."

"I know you want to be called George and the staff here know that too. But we have to be realistic."

I said nothing.

"It really doesn't matter what you call yourself or how you dress. We are entirely laid back about that sort of thing. And it really doesn't matter much that you pretend to have a Ph.D., though it does raise questions as to how far you are living in a fantasy world. What worries us, and others, is that there have been some unpleasant incidents recently, haven't there?"

I said nothing.

"Are you listening?"

All I heard was the bad voice in my head. It comes and it goes. I don't know why. And when it does, it tells me to do bad things.

"Josie, are you hearing voices?"

The bad voice told me to deny it. "I deny it."

The two medics exchanged looks.

"Josie, we think you ought to stay here for a time, maybe only for twenty-eight days, so that you can be assessed."

Then the bad voice reminded me that one of the best things about being dressed as a man is that you can conceal a stun gun and a pickaxe and a pile of bricks in your trouser pockets. *Attack your interrogators with all the weapons you have. Destroy them, destroy them.*

The medics must have seen the look in my eyes.

"Josie, don`t even think about it! We are here to help you. Now come with us. You really have no choice."

The bad voice seemed to drift away somehow, and so did the gun and the pickaxe and the bricks. I got up wearily. I felt empty. But I had to say something. Something that would hurt.

"Bastards!" I declared.

But they just smiled and nodded. "That`s good, Josie," the doctor said. "It shows you are reacting normally to what must be a stressful situation for you. Now come this way. The assessment centre is nearby."

We walked along the corridor. The receptionist-cum-nurse-cum-warder looked up and smiled. "Had a good visit, Doctor George?" She didn`t wait for an answer. "See you again soon."

I was a prisoner. Everyone must know that. The bad voice was back. *She is making fun of you. Get your revenge on her. Now! Now!*

I felt in my pocket for the stun gun, but it still wasn`t there.

So I just followed my gaolers. To the place where they would interrogate and torture me. I knew what they were thinking. That they could break me down. That I would soon be at their mercy. No way! Not me, a doctor of philosophy! They must be mad. Barking mad.

PUPPY LOVE

"Henry," the voice at the other end of the `phone was irritated. "Henry, are you listening to me?"

"Of course I am, dear," Henry replied, absentmindedly stroking the bare thigh of Francoise, the au pair, beside him. "You`ve just been telling me that your mother has taken a turn for the worse and you won`t be back until tomorrow. But why are you `phoning at eight o`clock on a Saturday morning? You know I am usually still asleep at this time."

The irritation at the other end became even more apparent. "It`s all right for you but I have been up half the night looking after Mother who, as you know, is not the easiest of people to deal with at the best of times. Not that you have seen her for Goodness knows how long. I just thought you might be interested to know what`s happening. I don`t suppose there is anything happening at your end?"

"Not a lot," Henry said, trying to keep the note of amusement out of his voice. "Louise spent most of yesterday evening doing her best to persuade me that we should buy her a puppy for her ninth birthday next week. Do you think we should?"

"Henry, we have talked about this before. She is far too young and completely irresponsible. We will have to think of something else."

At that moment, there was a loud knock at the bedroom door.

"Daddy, can I come in?"

Francoise shot out of bed like a wounded gazelle and disappeared into the en suite bathroom. Henry pulled the bed-clothes round himself. "Just a moment, Louise," he called, cupping the mouthpiece with one hand and then, to his wife, "Sorry, dear, I must ring off. There`s someone at the front door. Regards to your mother." He hung up.

Louise, uninvited, half opened the door and peered round.

"I have been looking for Francoise everywhere and I can`t find her."

"For Goodness` sake, why are you looking for her at this time of the morning?"

"Because I am bored and I want to play with her."

"It`s much too early in the morning to play with Francoise," Henry said, conscious of the irony of the situation. "Anyway, I think I heard her going out the front door so she has probably gone for a walk."

"She can`t have done. The front door is still bolted."

Henry searched round desperately for some explanation as to the mysterious disappearance of Francoise. "She may have gone out the back door."

"But that only leads into the garden," Louise objected, "and she is not there."

"I`m just going to have a shower. Go and have some breakfast. Then I`ll come down and we can look for her together." He spoke as though they lived in some vast mansion rather than in a three-bedroom terraced house.

Louise withdrew, disgruntled, slamming the door as she did so.

Francoise, still naked, emerged from the bathroom. "Do we `ave time for another ………..?" she began.

"No, certainly not. At least, not at the moment. Louise is on the war-path. You will have to think up some explanation as to where you`ve been."

"But `enry, what is it that I can say?"

"Say that you were in the study, writing a letter to your parents. And say it without batting an eyelid."

"What is this *batting an eyelid*? Is it a game English?"

"No, and it`s too difficult to explain now. Just try to appear convincing. I will go downstairs in a minute. You can follow a few minutes later."

When Henry entered the kitchen, Louise was engrossed in the television and was half-way through a plate of cornflakes and yoghurt. There was no mention of Francoise. For a few blissful moments Henry thought that she might have lost interest in the missing au pair. But when the latter came in, suitably dressed in jeans and a T-shirt, Louise looked up accusingly. "Where have you been hiding?"

"I have been in the stud. I have been doing the writing."

"If you mean the study, you weren`t. I looked."

Francoise glanced helplessly at Henry. "I will go get the newspapers," she announced, and for the second time that morning she shot out like a gazelle.

"I think," said Louise, carefully adjusting her large spectacles, "that she was in your bedroom."

Henry gave a convincing impression of being shocked. "Really, Louise! What on earth would she be doing there?"

"Doing what grown-ups do," Louise said laconically, scraping the bowl and licking the spoon, " I think it`s gross. I don`t see the point in it myself."

Henry instinctively adopted the language of a politician. "There is no truth in this disgraceful suggestion. I hope you will never raise the matter again."

"If there is no truth in it," Louise observed in a dead-pan sort of way, "then would it be all right if I tell Mummy when she gets back that Francoise disappeared and then seemed to come out of your bedroom?"

Henry paused to review his position. Then in a tightly controlled voice he said, "No, Louise it would not. Just forget it. What would you like to do today?"

"I want to go to the pet shop and for you to buy me a puppy. I am sure I will forget everything after that."

"Louise, this is blackmail."

"What is blackmail?" his daughter inquired, switching on her most innocent expression.

"Never you mind. All right, you win, though Goodness knows what your Mother will say when she learns that I have bought you a puppy. What sort do you want anyway?"

Louise was radiant. "I don`t mind as long as it is small and cuddly and has long ears and a long tail. And I want it to be a girl rather than a boy."

" I expect we can find something to meet your requirements," Henry said rather coldly. "Have you decided what you want to call her?"

Louise was in no doubt. "Yes, Francoise. It`s a nice name and it will remind me of the real Francoise for ages after she has gone." A sudden thought seemed to strike her. "And that will be nice for you too, Daddy, won`t it?"

COUNTRY AIR

The man stood gazing at the scene in front of him. At the green fields tinted a dull red by the setting sun, at the rutted country lane coated by the dry dust of a summer`s day, at the tall sweeping elms and gnarled oaks, at the majestic hills rolling into distance and obscurity.

He could almost sense the dampness of the mist which was creeping down to cover the night, and he fancied he could hear the whistle of a night bird or the flitting wings of a bat. And the stream that wound its way down from the heights seemed to be singing a song to itself, as though glad that dusk had come.

So near, yet so far in reality! He turned away from the moist canvass and plunged his brush into the jar of turpentine. Then he opened the studio window, breathed in the smoke and fumes of the City traffic, and tried to believe it was the pure country air that he loved.

A QUIET DAY

Betty cautiously dipped a ginger biscuit into her morning cup of Lady Grey tea. *So* much nicer than Earl Grey even though our dear Queen was said to drink nothing else. Well, Her Majesty couldn`t be right about everything, and anyway each person to their own taste. For all one knew, the Queen put milk into the cup first.

The `phone rang. Betty glanced at her watch. Eleven o`clock. So it would be Agnes, her best friend who phoned twice a day for a chat. Not that there was much to chat about. They were both widows, living a couple of miles apart in a quiet suburban area. The TV and the goings-on of their respective neighbours were their main sources of entertainment. Oh boredom! boredom! Betty occasionally thought to herself. But not a word to Agnes about that. One must keep up appearances.

"Is that you, Agnes?" she inquired unnecessarily. "How are you?" This was also unnecessary. Agnes was as fit as a fiddle, apart from the occasional arthritic twinge.

"Very well, dear. And how are you?"

"I am well, thank you. I`m just having a quiet day. What about you?"

Their chit-chat was eventually interrupted by the front door bell "I`ll ring off now, dear. There`s someone at the front door." Betty put the `phone down. Who could it be? Not another salesman peddling oven gloves and dusters?

She opened the door a few inches, protected by the chain, and peered out.

"It`s only me, Miss." It was Jeff the young window-cleaner who came every three months. She had quite forgotten he was due to visit her that day because she had quite forgotten to look at the kitchen calendar. She looked at him, and sniffed. The way he wore his hair in a coil! And his style in T-shirts! They always seemed to bear inscriptions that were, well, frankly not in good taste. But he had been cleaning the windows in her modest Edwardian terraced house for at least two years now, and his charges were quite reasonable by modern standards. Much less than Agnes paid, or so she said. Mind you, Agnes was always complaining about money. When she died, if ever, she would probably leave a small fortune.

"Come along in," Betty said. She was still grappling with her prejudices about the hair and the T-shirts. "Can I get you some tea?" She busied herself making a fresh pot. Then she poured out a cup, tea first, milk afterwards.

Jeff took a quick gulp. He almost choked. It tasted like cats` piss. Why couldn`t she make a decent cup of tea like everyone else?

A few minutes later he went upstairs, clutching his bucket and small step-ladder. Betty settled contentedly in her favourite chair in the lounge and opened The Daily Telegraph - *such* a good paper, not like those ghastly tabloids with rude pictures and things.

She was vaguely aware of a window being opened somewhere in the floor above as she studied a long article about Spanish fishermen and cod shortages. Then a shout and a crash. Instinctively, she looked out of the window, just in time to see a body falling past.

"Dear me!" she exclaimed. (It was not her practice to express herself in strong terms.) "That must be Jeff."

And so it was. He lay on his back in the small paved front garden next to the potted plants. He was splayed out and motionless and appeared to be either dead or nearly dead.

Betty had never had to dial 999 before. It was quite exciting.

Within minutes, paramedics and an ambulance and two police cars had arrived, and almost the whole street had come out to watch. Jeff was put onto a stretcher and carried into the ambulance. Everyone looked very serious. The ambulance sped away, its sirens blaring.

Betty offered a cup of tea to the young policewoman who took a statement from her. Two police officers went upstairs to inspect the window ledge. They came down a few minutes later with the bucket and step-ladder. "We`ll need these as exhibits," they explained. "For the time being, don't let anyone into that bedroom."

It was well after lunch-time when the police and crowds finally left. Betty heated up a Marks & Spencers' ready-made chicken pie before dozing off, the newspaper in her lap.

The 'phone rang. Betty roused herself. It was nearly four o'clock so it must be Agnes.

They inquired as to each other's health.

"I've had a busy day putting the rubbish out," Agnes announced. "What about you?"

"Oh, I've had a quiet day as usual. But we did have a bit of excitement. Jeff, he's the window-cleaner, came. He just sort of fell or dropped by and then he was carried off in an ambulance. I do hope he enjoyed the tea I gave him. I put something in it."

"Betty! What do you mean?"

"Well, my dear husband was, as you know, a pharmacist and when he unexpectedly left this world he also left some things behind in his cabinet. They are well past their shelf-life, of course, but they still seem to work."

"But Betty! This is dreadful. What on earth made you do it?"

"Oh, I don't know really. It just seemed a good idea at the time. I suppose I may need a new window-cleaner now. What's the name of your one?"

"I'm not sure I should tell you. I'm a bit shocked."

"Oh, don`t be so stuffy, Agnes! I wouldn`t do anything to your man, at least I don`t expect so. But come to think of it, I am just a bit worried about that young policewoman."

"What do you mean?"

"Well, I put something in her tea as well."

Agnes`s cry of horror at the end of the telephone was drowned by the sound of police sirens and the screech of car brakes.

Betty glanced out of the window. Grim-faced police officers were hurrying up the path to the front door. She gave one of her deep sighs. She was rather proud of her sighs. A good sigh could convey such a lot.

"Oh dear me, *visitors* !" she commented, as much to herself as to Agnes. "So inconsiderate of them to come uninvited, `specially as I was having a quiet day. But as it`s four o`clock, I wonder if I ought to offer them a cup of tea?"

WHERE`S THE BODY?

There was something odd about Palmerston Grove in Cockfosters. It was all to do with the residents of number 23. Everyone else in the street behaved nicely. They looked after each other`s cats when necessary, they took in parcels, they helped their neighbours in times of ill-health.

But not Leo and Bridget at number 23. They rarely spoke to anyone, they didn`t use the local shop, they kept themselves to themselves. If that had been all, no problem. But that was not all. For they were well known for the extraordinary frequency and loudness of their quarrels, often late into the night. Why they quarrelled and shouted at each other was a matter of speculation. At times, threats to kill could be heard.

Then one day Leo disappeared.

A couple of days passed before Bridget reported this to the police. According to her, he had left at 7.45 as usual for his office in the City. He had said nothing to suggest that he wouldn`t be home that evening but he failed to return. As a result half the shepherd`s pie had been wasted. She had not been unduly worried, however, because occasionally, after there had been a particularly strong "disagreement" (as she put it), he would stay overnight with a friend in Pimlico. It was only when she `phoned his office and was told that he had not been seen for two days that she began to think that something serious must have happened.

But the police were busy and showed little interest. After all, people went missing all the time. Usually they were good enough to turn up without wasting valuable police resources.

Bridget, however, was sure that Leo would never return. From her point of view this was fine. She could manage by herself and she would be spared his constant sarcasm and bad temper. Excellent! But then she made a bad mistake.

One Sunday afternoon, she took a pair of scissors and went to the wardrobe where he had kept his suits. Carefully, she took them off their hangers and slashed them to pieces. Cutting his only Savile Row pin-striped suit (admittedly a reject bought at a much reduced price) gave her particular pleasure. She bundled the remains into black bags and wrote out the letters RIP on a tag which she attached to one of the bags. A nice touch, she thought. Rest In Peace or perhaps Rest In Pieces or perhaps just Rip.

She gathered together the remainder of Leo`s possessions and stuffed them into more bags. Then she made her way to the far end of the garden and, with the aid of a large garden spade, dug a hole of sufficient depth to bury the lot. Good riddance! Afterwards, with the air of one who has done a useful day`s work, she retired to the kitchen for a welcome cup of tea.

The trouble was that Nora, a next door neighbour, had happened to be looking out of an upstairs window and had seen from behind the net curtains what was going on. That evening, she and her husband struggled briefly with their consciences. Of course they had no wish to be spiteful, Heaven forbid! But on the other hand, that cow Bridget deserved anything that was coming to her. They `phoned the police.

This time the police took the matter seriously. After all, most murders are committed by spouses or by people living together. (No point in living together unless you have at least some of the advantages and disadvantages of married life.) And Leo and Bridget were, or at least had been, married. So that was that. A search warrant was obtained and the garden was turned over. The remains of Leo`s clothes and possessions were unearthed although regrettably, as the police and later the Crown Prosecution Service thought, there were no signs of Leo himself. But there was evidence of threats to kill, the strange disappearance of Leo, and the fact that his mutilated clothes and other possessions had been found in the garden.

In the bleak early hours of a November morning, two senior police officers rang the front door bell, and Bridget`s nightmare began. The whole thing was surreal. The warrant for arrest on a charge of murder, the long hostile interviews, the cells, the squalor, the interminable wait until the Trial.

The Trial itself. The Defence had one obviously strong point: where`s the body? But the Prosecution said that if the Defendant was callous enough to cut up her husband`s clothes and write RIP on a tag and bury all his possessions, she was callous enough to murder him, quite apart from the threats to kill. And Bridget did badly in the witness box. No signs of remorse at destroying the clothing and no signs of regret at Leo`s disappearance.

In the end, after a long retirement and by a majority of 10 to 2, the jury found her guilty. She was sentenced to life imprisonment. There stretched ahead an eternity of iron bars and prison cells, the monotony of a life without purpose, sheer grey misery.

~~~~~~~~~~

At about the same time, somewhere in South America, Leo was sunning himself beside the swimming pool of a large villa.

Next to him lounged the strikingly good-looking dark, immensely wealthy woman he was living with. She watched him thoughtfully, her Armani sun-glasses perched on her forehead. The man was a complete bastard of course but for some reason he amused her. And she was getting used to that stupid little beard he was trying to grow. Oh well, when she got tired of him she would with any luck manage to pass him over to her sister who lived in Chile and was a sucker for Englishmen. Now, what was he saying?

"Do you know, I've been thinking. I think I might send a picture postcard to Bridget, just to say *Having a great time. Glad you're not here*. That should cause a bit of a stir back home."

She laughed. "I wouldn't if I were you. From what you've told me about her I don't suppose she cares a fig where you are."

"You could be right. Not worth the cost of the stamp. It was just an idea." Lazily he helped himself to a third tequila. "You know, life for me was sheer misery in England, apart from our fun times in your pad in Pimlico. I've never said this to you before but thank you for rescuing me. Ever since I came here, I've felt this fantastic sense of what can I say, yes, I know, *freedom*."

She nodded, and raised her glass. "Let's drink to that."

They clinked glasses.

"To Freedom."

PARLOUR GAMES

The building might once have been a shop. Now it had blue shutters and a sign, *The Handy Sauna and Massage Parlour*. Harold glanced quickly to right and left. Nobody in sight. He took a deep breath, pushed open the front door and went in.

The reception area was small, lit by a single neon light. A faint antiseptic smell hung in the air, a mixture of hospital ward and indoor swimming-pool. Behind the low counter, a woman was concentrating on painting her fingernails bright green. Crow-black hair, Gothic-style eye make-up and thick red lip-stick. A crumpled overall which once upon a time could have been white.

She looked up and switched on a smile that was probably meant to be welcoming. "Hallo, darling, and what can we do for you?" Her voice was husky, the voice of a heavy smoker.

"I want a massage."

"Yes, darling. What sort do you want?" Then, suspiciously. "I haven`t seen you before. You`re not the Bill, are you?"

"A policeman! For God`s sake! Do I look like one?"

She relaxed. "No, you don`t, but you`re not one of our regulars, like, and I have to be careful. It`s a funny old world. What`s your name?"

Harold hesitated.

"It don`t have to be your real name. Just what you want us to call you, like. I am Susie."

Harold wondered whether that was her real name. He thought quickly. "Rupert." (He hoped his daughter`s hamster wouldn`t mind.)

"That`s a nice name. I`ll call you Rup. Okay, you can have a look at this." She rummaged under the desk and handed over a card. A large menu, made out in spiky handwriting.

Amazing! If he ever got the chance, he would shop around and see what other massage parlours had to offer.

"What`s a Top Special? It`s very pricey."

"You get everything, like," Susie replied. "It should keep you going for days. It`s worth it. And you can have any girl you want."

"But I only want a straight massage."

Susie looked scandalised. "Straight massage! You must be joking. We don`t do *that* sort of thing here."

They were interrupted by a noisy altercation going on in the background. A man`s voice was raised. "I want my money back." A woman`s voice, "Well, you can`t have it."

Then the sound of a scuffle. Two people were coming down the narrow stairs towards the reception area. The woman was saying, "I`ve done my bit. I can`t help it if you`re not up to it." The man was struggling to put on his clothes. At the same time he was trying to push her away.

He was tall and young, in his twenties. Harold caught a glimpse of the woman. She was tugging the man's shirt.

Susie saw Harold's expression. "It's all right, Rup. Don't you worry. We get some funny people in here, like, but our girls are the best, they'll do anything you want. Much better than a straight massage."

Harold had seen enough. "Sorry, I have to go." He bolted out into the street.

He walked quickly to a grey Vauxhall parked in a nearby side street. He sat thoughtfully in the driver's seat and then began to make notes. Two minutes later, the young man joined him, out of breath. He grinned at Harold. "Okay, Sarge! I had a bit of trouble with that tom but I reckon I've got the evidence we need. It's a knocking-shop all right."

Harold was cautious, unusually so for him. "Yeah, but that doesn't mean our evidence will stick if we ever get to court. Now back to base! I could do with a cuppa. We can make our notes up in the canteen. Just don't jump over the nearest bridge if Higher Authority decides not to prosecute. Leave it with me."

He looked at the younger officer with amusement. "And how's this plain-clothes work suiting you?"

"It's all right for you. I'm the one who has to take my clothes off!"

Back at the massage parlour, a slanging match was going on between Susie and the other girl. "I don't know what the fuck is wrong with you! That's two punters you've fucking well lost us. The first guy didn`t get what he wanted and then you fucking well shout at him and scare the other one off."

"Go and fuck yourself," the girl replied disagreeably. "Anyway, you said the second guy only wanted a straight massage."

Susie`s anger evaporated. She laughed, and lit a cigarette. "I saw through that crap. He would have come round, like, given a bit more time. I guess I would have talked him in to having a Top Special."

"I bet you wouldn`t. He was just sussing us out. I know him. He`s the Bill."

"Never!"

"He is. His name is Harold. He`s married. With kids. A regular punter of mine on my old patch. And the things he got up to! If he tries to have a go at us in court, I can string him up by his balls. And he knows it. He saw me on them stairs. He won`t play no more games with us, don`t you worry."

Susie thoughtfully exhaled a stream of smoke.

"So no hassle, then? That`s good. Looks like he`s screwed himself up, good and proper, the little darling. Funny old world."

HARD TIMES

Mike shifted uncomfortably on the hard pavement. He felt grubby and dispirited. He`d only collected a couple of pounds the whole morning. And it was starting to rain. Shit! Shit! Shit!

"So what`s your problem?"

Standing over him was a thin, middle-aged woman with small spectacles, a prissy voice and greying hair tied in a bun. Oh God! But he could hardly ignore her. Though she looked like a school teacher she was expensively dressed. Perhaps financial salvation had arrived.

He put on his ingratiating whine. "I`ve fallen on hard times and I`m skint and homeless and hungry."

"Then come home with me. I`ll give you some sort of meal and a roof over your head."

Shit! Who did she think she was? Some stupid do-gooder? "No, lady," he said. "Very kind of you, I`m sure, but I couldn`t put you to that trouble. If you could just spare a bit of change………….."

"No, I won`t do that . But if you come with me, I`ll give you twenty pounds and you don`t have to stay the night."

Jesus! If passers-by heard that, what the hell would they think? A pervert! But she didn`t look the type. Not like that Madam Maisie, with all her gear. Mike gave a slight shudder.

"And you are obviously cold. So come along with me. I`ve got a car in the car-park two minutes` away." She was almost pleading with him.

Mike was tempted. Food and twenty pounds sounded like good news and beggars can`t be choosers, he told himself. He could always escape if things got too hot. Besides, he`d had a miserable morning and it was raining, and the hostel kept its doors shut until five o`clock.

"All right," he said, gathering his few possessions together. "But I`m a bit smelly. Haven`t had a bath for a few days."

The woman laughed. "Don`t worry. I`m not troubled."

They walked in silence to the car-park. The woman drew out her keys and the amber lights flashed on a large silver-coloured Mercedes. "Get in, we don`t have far to go."

Mike climbed in, chucked his possessions onto the rear seat and struggled with the seat-belt. She leant over him. "Can I help? Phew! Yes, you do ponk. Never mind."

She drove expertly. A few minutes later they pulled up outside a mock-Georgian house in a tree-lined avenue. He followed her uncertainly into the house.

"You really must have a bath now," she said. "You can use the one on the second floor."

Mike wondered whether there was any point in protesting. Probably not. Better do what he was told. He made his way up the stairs and went into the bathroom which was large and elegant. He tried to lock the door but the lock didn`t work. Oh well, here goes, he thought, and soon he was luxuriating in the hot bath and trying out the different sorts of bath essence.

The door suddenly opened. Shit! But surprise! surprise! It wasn`t the same woman who came through the doorway but a much younger woman, little more than a girl. And she was only wearing a towel casually draped round herself. "Hi! Don`t look so alarmed," she said, her voice full of amusement. "It`s not what you think. This is a very respectable house."

"You could have fooled me," Mike said. "I just came here for some food and some cash and I end up in a bath and then a girl barges in wearing nothing more than a towel."

The girl laughed. "Yes, put like that it might seem a bit odd. But I guess Mum decided that you are an okay sort of bloke even though you`re living rough. I wouldn`t like you to think that she makes a habit of inviting beggars back home. One has to be careful these days, doesn`t one?"

"Yes, I suppose one does," Mike agreed cautiously. "But would you mind telling me what this is all about?"

"Oh, come on, Dad! It`s weeks since you walked out, and Mum just happened to see you in the street and took pity on you. Now would you grab a towel and get out of the bath please because I want to have a shower? And try and make it up with Mum. We`ve both missed you." Unexpectedly, a tear trickled down one cheek. "Since you left, it`s as though we have fallen on hard times."

"I know that feeling," Mike said.

CECIL AND THE TENTH COMMANDMENT

Without his dog-collar, Cecil looked entirely undistinguished. Thirty years ago when he had been ordained he had had the Faith but somehow this had diminished with the passage of time. Now it had almost vanished and only the daily routine and modest respect paid to him as a man of the Cloth kept him going.

Over the breakfast table in the country vicarage, Cecil looked up from The Daily Telegraph. "According to a recent poll," he observed, "78% of people still believe in marriage as an institution, 42% believe that bestiality should be a good ground for divorce as distinct from 30% for adultery, 28% cruelty, and 15% incompatibility."

Hilda looked across at his scrawny neck without enthusiasm. "What about desertion?" The tone of her voice suggested that she had been thinking about this for years.

Cecil turned over a page and cautiously adjusted his rimless spectacles. "It doesn`t say."

"Of course it must say. It is one of the main reasons why marriages bust up."

Cecil returned to the previous page. "You're quite right," he said, "or at least you're partly right. It is headed *Grounds for Divorce other than Desertion*."

They looked at each other with mutual dislike.

"In view of the emphasis on bestiality," Cecil observed, "I think I had better make it my main text for the sermon on Sunday."

"I am not sure that your tiny congregation will appreciate that," Hilda said. "You have only got nine regulars and they are all aged at least seventy. I can't imagine that Matilda, who must be eighty-five if she is a day, would even understand let alone take on board the merits or de-merits of bestiality."

"I don't agree," Cecil said, his voice rising slightly as a display of clerical authority. "It is a great mistake to assume that people of advanced years don't have a good understanding of human nature or, come to think of it, animal behaviour. Anyway, Matilda can't hear a thing."

"All right, you win," said Hilda unpleasantly, " but if your congregation gets even smaller we shall all be out of a job. And what is your text going to be: the Tenth Commandment?"

"Coveting your neighbour's ass was never meant to refer to bestiality," he said primly, "I need something better and more immediate than that." However, he thought, Hilda's idea was really rather good and if he used it there would be no need to waste time in thought and research. He retired to his so-called study which he used largely as a retreat from the irritations of domestic life and jotted down a few notes for the sermon.

When the moment came on Sunday, he advanced to the pulpit with the faint sense of excitement that still affected him. The thought of speaking on a subject of one`s own choice for ten or fifteen minutes or more to a largely uncomprehending audience had a certain fascination. At least those members of the congregation who were not completely deaf usually seemed to listen for the first couple of minutes before attention wandered or evaporated completely.

As he entered the pulpit on this occasion, he noticed that the small regular congregation had unexpectedly swelled by the late arrival of a weekend-cottage husband and wife and their two young children. Shit! The sermon was entirely unsuitable but there was no time to go back. Cecil decided to deal with the situation by increasing the unctuous tone of his voice.

"My text this morning is quite simply the Tenth Commandment but with the emphasis on the ass and the ox. Most of us remember the first few Commandments but how many of us can recite all of them? When we speak of loving our neighbours, we do not necessarily mean loving them in the carnal sense. There is more to it than that. It must depend upon the circumstances and indeed upon the particular neighbour. So is it with the beasts in the field."

He looked up from his almost illegible notes and surveyed the congregation. Betty, an old stalwart, was just beginning to nod off but this was par for the course. Onwards!

"Many of us feel, and feel strongly, that marriage is a sacred institution. It has been described as the bedrock of our civilization. But we know, sadly do we not, that many a marriage and indeed a marriage bed, entered into with enthusiasm and hope, founder almost before one can say Jack Robinson. There are many reasons for this. One, according to a recent poll conducted by a National newspaper, is quite simply *bestiality*."

Did he detect a sudden flicker of interest among the congregation? Certainly Betty appeared to have woken up with a start.

"What does that mean? As all of you will know or," he added hastily, catching a gleam of outrage in the eyes of the husband and wife team, "as most of you will know, it means connection or attempted connection, depending on size and circumstance, between man and beast. In this context the word man probably means man rather than woman but not necessarily so. After all, we are but one in the eyes of God.

"Clearly there is too much of this sort of thing going on. Too many marriages are sliding downhill because of it." He peered down at his haphazard notes and was quite unable to read the next entry. "Praise be to God," he improvised smoothly. "And we must spare a thought, must we not, for the animals themselves who, leaving aside those of a peculiarly savage disposition, are defenceless against the ravages of men and possibly women? Whether it is the love of the British people for animals large and small which has led to bestiality being regarded so seriously at least in relation to marriage is a matter of speculation. But let us not speculate. Let us not think either of the other reasons why marriages come to an end, such as desertion, adultery, cruelty and others that may spring to mind. I hope to deal with all these, not necessarily in order of merit, in sermons yet to come.

"In the meanwhile, should we not also have compassion for all our fellow-beings who favour this bestial behaviour, if bestial behaviour it be? It is all too easy to throw glass stones." Surely that couldn`t be right. Oh well! Too late to do anything about it. "We must turn the other cheek. We must accept that we all, or almost all, have animal instincts. But we must not let them get the better of us. Above all, we must not let bestiality dominate our thoughts. And so I end as I began, thinking as I do and you do too or so I trust, about the Tenth Commandment, and let us, in the silence of this congregation, acknowledge among ourselves that we respect our bodies, male or female, regardless of sex, colour or religion.

"And now in the name of the Father, Son and Holy Ghost, let us join together and lift up our voices and sing the hymn All Things Bright and Beautiful. You may like to know that this week the connection, I beg your pardon, the collection, is in aid of the local home for lost stray dogs and cats."

I think that went quite well, Cecil said to himself as he descended from the pulpit. Pity about the gaffe in respect of the collection. Never mind, you can`t get everything right the whole time. Pity also, he reflected shortly afterwards, about the almost absurdly small size of the collection. Tough luck on you stray dogs and cats. Never mind! He made his way to the church door so as to shake hands and say farewell to the departing guests. They invariably departed in the same order which made it easier to remember who had what ailments.

"And how is the leg today? Oh! What a shame! Perhaps it will be better next week. God be with you. And how is the arthritis today? Oh! What a shame! God be with you. Perhaps it will be better next week."

The second eldest member of the congregation paused, as always, to say, "Thank you for that sermon. What an inspiration!" And as always, Cecil replied, "Thank you, I`m so glad you found it helpful." On this occasion he resisted the temptation to add, I had no idea you were so interested in bestiality.

The husband and wife team, however, bundled their children past him with averted eyes. The husband, white in the face, ignored the proferred hand and said in a tightly-controlled voice, "That was a disgrace. An absolute disgrace. I shall report you to the Bishop."

"I wouldn't do that if I were you," said Cecil evenly, "The Bishop happens to live near a zoo and there is an investigation going on at this very minute about his relationship with a koala bear."

The husband gave a squawk of horror and bolted down the path.

Cecil looked upwards. What he had said about the Bishop was entirely untrue but it appeared to have done the trick. "Good Lord, thank you for the inspiration," he murmured.

Quite suddenly, his Faith had returned.

WHAMBO

The healthy lifestyle with something extra for all ages

Your main **exercise** for the day starts at 5 am when you set out for your 2 hour Whambo run. Combine running, skipping and jumping. Remember to stop every 10 minutes to emit loud animal cries which are so necessary to assist with your breathing. You will soon become impervious to the glances, comments and curious gestures of other road-users.

Your **diet** will start as soon as you return from the run. Use 2 litres of buffalo milk to make fresh healthy yoghurt. Remember to add a dash of garlic. Later at work you can have a sip of life-enhancing linseed oil and for lunch a small portion of fish which is past its prime. (Fresh fish is harmful because it may induce a desire for more.) Supper is the main meal of the day and consists entirely of yoghurt though for a real treat you can wash this down with parsley sauce rounded off with an overripe banana.

Throughout the day you should **relax** every 15 minutes by standing up, closing your eyes and placing both hands lightly on top of your head. If relaxation is not practicable (for example when driving a car or riding a motor-cycle) be sure to make up for lost time as soon as you can. Try to close your mind to what people around you are saying. In the late evening when your neighbours are idly watching television or trying to sleep, you must practise your musical-instrument, preferably the trombone, for a full hour.

As for **self recognition** you will soon appreciate that you have become a different person and that your partner (if you still have one), relatives, friends and colleagues now look at you in a new light. This is quite simply because they are envious. Deal with any apparent criticism by remaining completely silent and by shaking your head vigorously. Coincidentally this itself is an effective form of exercise and relaxation.

Well done! Later in the programme we will discuss **self-defence**. You may find this useful……….

NAKED AMBITION

Sir Charles Monkford, one of Her Majesty's High Court judges, lay back in his bath, scratching his balls.

His wife Cynthia unexpectedly popped her head round the door. "Er, don't do that, dear," she exclaimed. "What's worrying you?"

"I think I've made too many decisions against the Government recently," Charles said. "Of course we are all independent and entitled to do our own thing as it were but I can't help feeling it may scupper my chances of promotion."

"That's silly. You're a dead cert to get to the Court of Appeal. But if you're really worried about it, why don't you have a word with the Bruiser?"

"I do wish you wouldn't call the Lord Chief Justice that. It wasn't his fault that an angry litigant threw a garden gnome at him and broke his nose."

"I never understood why there was a garden gnome in the court at all."

"It was an important exhibit I believe, but anyway I would still prefer it if you just called him the Chief."

"That makes him sound like an Indian warrior," Cynthia protested, "but if you like we could invite him and the

Dragoness to dinner and you could have a quiet chat with him when he's on his fourth brandy."

Charles silently debated whether to object to the description Dragoness but decided against it. After all, it was entirely accurate. Duty required him, however, to spring to the defence of the Chief. "You make him sound like an alcoholic, as it were. I doubt if he will have more than one glass."

"So you agree we should have them to dinner? All right, I'll see if I can make the arrangements. I'll speak to the Dragoness. And it's time you got out of the bath. You don't want your genitals to drop off."

After dinner a fortnight later, the two men were sitting contentedly in Charles's study. Lord Oakley the Chief was halfway through his third glass of Remy Martin. Charles decided the right moment had come.

"I wonder if I could mention something that's been troubling me?" he murmured. "You see, I have this uneasy impression that I have made too many decisions against the Government recently and I really don't want to be, well, held back in any way because of that. I just wanted to test the waters with you, as it were."

The Chief exploded with laughter. "You old fox. That's why you invited us to dinner. Well I can set your mind at rest. No one is remotely interested in the idea that you may have found against the Establishment from time to time. It's just not relevant when it comes to deciding who should be elevated to the Court of Appeal."

Charles gave an audible sigh of relief. "Well, that`s really good to hear. So I`m in with a chance, as it were?"

"No offence, old boy, but you haven`t got a cat`s hope in hell. You are fairly okay as a judge of fact but you don`t have a reputation as a good lawyer. Just be content with your lot, my dear chap, and stuff your ambitions. Do you mind if I have another glass of your excellent brandy?"

An hour or so later, Cynthia unexpectedly popped her head round the bathroom door. "Er, don`t do that, dear."

HELP YOURSELF

"Let's talk about your relationship with your step-father when you were young," Caroline said briskly, eyeing her patient across the table.

A rash of red spots suddenly appeared round Amanda's neck. "He was horrible towards me."

"In what way?" Caroline inquired.

"He never liked me, you know. He resented me. He hardly ever spoke to me. He tried to pretend I wasn't there."

"I seem to remember you told me that he used to take you, your mother and two step-brothers away together on holidays most years." Caroline had acquired the psychotherapists' knack of reading from her notes whilst maintaining eye-contact with her patient.

"He did," Amanda agreed reluctantly. "At Easter he rented a caravan near Bognor Regis and in August he drove us down to a damp little villa in the Dordogne."

"You must have talked to each other quite a lot on those occasions?" Caroline explored gently.

"You don't believe me, do you?" Amanda said, tears coming into her eyes. "He ignored me as best he could."

Caroline pushed the box of tissues across the table. "Did *you* try to talk to him?"

"Not unless I had to. And if I did, one or other of my step-brothers would interrupt and try to prevent me."

Caroline was momentarily intrigued. "Remind me, how old were they?"

"Well, when my mother re-married, I was eleven and they were three and five but they got older of course."

"Yes, I suppose they would have done." Caroline suppressed a wild desire to giggle. "But you got on quite well with them, didn`t you, apart from that incident when you threw them into the swimming-pool?"

"I`d forgotten I had told you about that." Amanda dabbled her eyes with another tissue. "I was only twelve at the time and I`m sure I didn`t mean to drown them. Anyway, they were rescued quite soon."

"I expect your step-father was rather upset about it."

"He was. He went right over the top. He showed no understanding. He didn`t even *try* to understand."

Amanda gave a theatrical gesture and buried her head in her hands.

Oh God ! Caroline thought, glancing surreptitiously at her watch. Another thirty minutes to go. "What I think we should do is to discuss your present feelings about him. I sense that they are not entirely negative. Shall we try to look at them in a positive sort of way?"

Half-an-hour later, Caroline and Amanda had more or less disposed of the step-father.

While Amanda wrote out a cheque, Caroline emptied the waste-paper basket. "I think we are making real progress, don't you?" she said brightly. "Next week, we can talk again about your mother. I want you to tell me more about how you got on together before your third marriage and the incident with the Tango."

As Amanda left, Caroline made some brief notes and looked at her appointments diary. She sighed and got up to move the patients' chair further away. Alcoholics could be a nuisance at times and Philip, her next client, usually arrived smelling heavily of whisky.

How long can I go on with this work? Caroline asked herself. It's only ten o'clock in the morning but I need something stronger than coffee. She unlocked the bottom drawer of her desk and withdrew a bottle of vodka. She poured herself a generous amount and added a dash of orange-juice.

A minute later there was a bang on the door and Philip staggered through. More by luck than good judgement he managed to slump into the chair without knocking it over.

Caroline switched on her professional smile of welcome.

"How nice to see you again! But there is something we must discuss straightaway. Why do you always seem to need a strong drink before coming to see me?"

CLUBBING

He looked at his teenage daughter with distaste. The dress was absurdly short, the midriff was bare, and the shoes were pink stilettos.

"And where are you off to tonight?"

"Clubbing."

"Whale cubs, I suppose."

"Dad! Don`t be gross! You like clubs yourself."

"I hardly think that the Streatham Rotary Club bears much resemblance to the sort of club you favour. And when I go there, I certainly don`t dress to kill."

"You do when you slope off to your Masonic Club. I caught you trying on your kit in front of the mirror last week, so don`t be so stuffy."

He decided to change tack. "And who are you going with?"

"I don`t see it`s any of your business, but if you must know it`s Andy."

"Is he the one with the----?"

"Yes."

"It may not be any of my business, but I must say I preferred that boy, what was his name, Chris?"

"It`s all over with him, and I`m not going to tell you why."

"When will you be back?"

"I don`t know. I may go on somewhere afterwards."

"Somewhere! Somewhere! Couldn`t you be a bit more specific?"

"No, how can I be when I don`t know myself?"

"All right, all right, off you go, but look after yourself. And don`t be too late."

He watched his daughter flounce out of the front door and waited a few moments. Then he dialled for a mini-cab. "As soon as possible, please." He lowered his voice. "To the Streatham Strip Club."

THE CHRISTMAS SPIRIT

Everyone agreed that it had been a perfectly awful family Christmas. Except Nicholas, aged 7, who thought it had been brilliant. He had got the festivities off to a rousing start on Christmas Eve by asking in a loud voice why the wart on Granny`s nose had got so much bigger. He was a bright boy and was relying upon his innocent expression and apparent search for knowledge to carry him through. It did, just. But Granny stormed off to her room saying that she needed to lie down because of the horrendous pains in her back and left hip and she doubted whether, at her age, she would be fit to take any further part in the celebrations.

Grand-dad appeared to be intensely amused by the incident and waved his arms about in appreciation. His mental faculties had gone downhill years ago and he was now often difficult to understand. On this occasion he made himself clear. "Got it in one, got it in one!" he exclaimed, in Nicholas`s direction. This was one of his favourite phrases and dated back nearly 20 years when he had claimed (contrary to the evidence) to have holed in one when playing golf.

A number of incidents marred the success of Christmas Day itself. The task of wrapping up the presents and attaching gift labels had unwisely been left to Uncle Cyril the night before. Inevitably he managed to get many of these mixed up, due to his policy of abstinence in respect of attendance at meetings of Alcoholics Anonymous as well as his off-beat sense of humour. The children by and large received the presents which had been intended for them though for Emma, aged 9, an adult video misleadingly called "Puss in Boots" had to be seized and replaced by the more suitable "Dick Whittington". In relation to himself, Uncle Cyril had skilfully substituted a bottle of whisky for the calendar which had been chosen for him. A generous-sized box of chocolates was given to cousin Edith who was diabetic and a dog-collar to Fiona who kept cats. More provocatively, a pair of thongs clearly designed for the male physique was presented to Granny instead of to Uncle David and the latter received the shawl intended for her. Finally, Grand-dad was mistakenly given a kitchen rolling-pin which he wielded with great glee until it was forcibly removed from him. He then dissolved into floods of tears until Emma kindly lent him her newly-acquired toy elephant. He played with this happily for the rest of the day despite the efforts of Jessica (aged 8 and in a tantrum because she had not been given a mobile-phone) to sever the animal`s trunk.

Sarah had many attributes as a mother but they stopped some distance short of the kitchen. Lunch was not a success. The turkey was burnt to a cinder and whatever had been used for stuffing gave off an offensive smell which Jessica said was like poo. The vegetables had lost all sense of identity. The Christmas pudding looked and tasted like a mud-pie. Even the traditional pulling of crackers was spoilt by the more elderly members of the family complaining about their arthritic wrists but resenting any offer of help. Nicholas pointed out that Uncle Cyril`s red hat matched the colour of his face. Uncle Cyril retaliated by claiming that the port was corked and then managed to drop the decanter. Fiona broke a tooth on a walnut and looked accusingly at Sarah who burst into tears. The cat vomited over Edith.

The dish-washer had broken down the day before. Nobody was willing to help with the washing-up. Squabbling among the children as to which TV programme to watch led to a physical fight requiring first-aid to Jessica`s neck. Simmering dislike between the adults ended with an unpleasant altercation by the men as to the rival merits of Arsenal and Manchester United and by the women as to the respective merits of their various children. Eventually the men went outside in search of a restorative drink, possibly from a vat in Uncle Cyril`s car outside, and came back later in an even more aggressive mood. The children were sent to bed early. The adults bickered as to the choice of TV programme. Granny declared that there was no point in looking at anything at all now that they had missed The Queen.

Despite the pile of unwashed dishes that spread round the kitchen like debris from a shipwreck, Boxing Day started well enough but rapidly went downhill when cousin Lisa and her friend Karen arrived. Their relationship had been the subject of gossip for months. They had decided that this was the day when they would "come out" publicly. But as they arrived at the door, Nicholas who had been watching through the window exclaimed loudly that he had just seen them kissing. They were so thrown by this that they instinctively denied it. After that, they felt that any announcement would seem silly and so had better be postponed. Nicholas`s remarkable command of English sometimes let him down and so his comment that he didn`t care if Lisa and Karen were a couple of thespians caused a mixture of hilarity and outrage. The children were all banished to another room where they were later discovered watching intently the video "Puss in Boots".

Over the lunch-table, Granny radiated disapproval at Lisa and Karen and at the whole Christmas experience. Nicholas toyed with the idea of making some reference to her cheerfulness but sensibly decided that he had chanced his luck as far as he could. His turn came later. He was playing quietly with a new but old-fashioned toy called "Jungle Set" which imaginatively included a box of small darts to be projected at approaching wild beasts. Uncle Cyril, who had consumed 3 bottles of supermarket claret, rose unsteadily and leant over the mock log fire in an attempt to increase the size of the flames by blowing into them. His capacious bottom was no more than 6 feet from Nicholas who almost instinctively discharged one of the darts. It struck its target amidships. Uncle Cyril gave a squawk and pitched forward into the fire.

Grand-dad, who had been watching closely, was delighted. "Got it in one!" he announced, and then, with a rare extension of his vocabulary, "When`s next Christmas?"

Quite clearly, Nicholas was not the only one to have had a brilliant Christmas.

SAVANNAH HEAT

In the middle of the night, Harry and Martha lay naked back to back in their hotel king-size bed in the historic district of Savannah, Georgia. They were naked simply because the air-conditioning was defective. Physical relationships had ceased some years previously after an incident when Harry had run his Ford truck over and killed Martha`s iguana, Boris. Martha maintained that this had been deliberate. Harry had always denied this but agreed that he had never liked Boris. The jury remained out but the marriage had never been the same since.

An objective observer, looking down into the hotel bedroom, would have been forgiven for saying that the scene was frankly unattractive. Harry, aged 57, and turning bald, was short and obese. Martha, slightly younger, was tall and thin to an extent bordering upon anorexia. Even when asleep, her face bore a perpetually pinched expression. Fortunately, there was of course no observer, objective or otherwise. But it was on this scene that disaster, of a sort, was about to strike.

The couple`s slumbers were shattered as the hotel fire-alarm system went off. "It`s a fire", Harry declared, leaping out of bed. The alarm stopped. "Maybe it was a false alarm," Martha, still half-asleep, suggested.

Harry cautiously opened the bedroom door and sniffed. "I can smell burning, it's the real thing. Don't be spooked. I'll take care of this. We can't risk using the elevator. We will have to go down the stairs."

"We must put some clothes on and take some of our stuff. We can't go like this."

"Listen to me." Harry was always at his best, in his view at least, in times of crisis. "We don't have any time." Unexpectedly he seized the bed sheets and plunged them under the shower. He wrapped one round himself and handed the other to his wife.

"But I must take my mink coat," Martha wailed.

"There's no time for anything." Harry was on his way to the door. Then he remembered that the mink coat was uninsured. "OK, put it on quick."

The hotel corridor was silent. "If there really is a fire," Martha said, "why isn't the alarm still ringing and why aren't people hurrying to leave?"

"They are probably burning to death," Harry replied, ignoring the first point. Together they struggled awkwardly down the stairs.

The night clerk, tall, black and of immense dignity, switched off the television-set behind the reception desk and stood up as they came in to sight. He showed no surprise at seeing two frightened-looking guests wearing only wet sheets and, in relation to the wife, a partly concealed fur coat.

"Can I help you?"

"Where`s the fire?" Harry demanded.

"I am really sorry about this, we don`t have a fire. Someone was fixing themselves a hot dog and it kinda got out of hand and set the smoke-alarm off. I guess if it had been a real fire the alarm would have kept on ringing and there would be folk all over the place trying to get out."

Martha shot a triumphant look at her husband but in view of his expression wisely decided not to say, I told you so.

"This is crazy. I will decide who I am going to complain to in the morning." Abruptly, Harry turned and began to make his way towards the stairs.

"Why not take the elevator?" the clerk suggested helpfully, his eyes on the little trail of water emanating from the wet sheets. "You`ll find it more comfortable than climbing three flights of stairs. It`s not as though we`ve had a real fire."

In silence the couple ascended to the third floor but Harry became loudly vocal on finding that the bedroom door had locked itself when they had left. "There`s no good you swearing," Martha said sharply, "You`d better go down again and get that clerk to give you another key."

"I will do no such thing. Do you think I`m going to spend the whole night waltzing about this god-damned place in a wet sheet looking like a dumb penguin?" To Martha`s surprise, he charged at the door which split open with a crash.

They went in quickly. Harry tried to put the broken panels back into position and shut the door as best he could. As the lock no longer worked, he opened the door again and carefully hung the "*Do not disturb*" sign on the handle outside.

Martha had removed her sheet and was drying herself vigorously with a towel. Incongruously, she was still wearing the fur coat. Looking at her, Harry was suddenly struck with an urge he had not felt in relation to her for years.

"Honey," he said uncertainly, "I kinda think that after all this time, maybe we could make things up between us. Do you think we might ……….?"

At that moment there was a loud knock at the door.

"It`s the night manager, sir. Could I speak with you?"

Harry twisted a towel round himself and opened the door a few inches. "Can`t you see the *Do not disturb* sign?" he snarled.

The night manager, a young man wearing shorts and a T-shirt, was unperturbed. "Yes sir, and we have strict instructions never to disturb our guests unless there is an exceptional reason. And as I have had a report that two guests in this room have been seen walking along the corridors in wet sheets, and one or possibly both of them in a fur jacket underneath, I guess this is exceptional. It certainly doesn`t happen every night. And have you had some problem with your door?" His voice was calm but he seemed to be having difficulty in keeping a straight face.

Harry decided that the best line of defence was to attack. "This is just stupid. The fire-alarm went off. We had to take care of ourselves. You`ve made us look even more stupid. Tomorrow, I will find a lawyer and sue the hotel."

"Sure," said the manager equably, "My brother is an attorney right here in town. I will give you his card. I have to apologise to you folks and at this time I will arrange for you to have a complimentary breakfast in the morning at our expense. Have a great night and a nice day."

With the door more-or-less shut once more, Harry turned towards Martha. The emotions he had felt a minute or two before had subsided. "You know, Honey, perhaps it is not such a good idea to sue the hotel. I guess in court we could be made out to look like a couple of jerks. Let`s just settle for that free breakfast."

"Do you figure it will be a hot breakfast?"

"Sure, Honey, everything is hot in Savannah!"

MUSICAL CHAIRS

The specially invited audience sat expectantly in the elegant concert hall. The chance of seeing and hearing the famous concert pianist on one of his rare visits to London was a prize almost beyond imagination.

Adrian, the assistant box-office manager, now seated to one side of the platform, felt differently. In fact he was in a complete state of terror. For only two minutes before, he had received a message in an uneven scrawl from the master of ceremonies. "Adrian, I`m pissed. You do the introduction and vote of thanks."

Unhappily, Adrian had little musical knowledge. A second problem was that his mind had gone a complete blank as to the name and identity of the guest. Thirdly, he couldn`t remember anything about the forthcoming music. And it was too late to find out.

A crackle of excitement followed by loud applause from the audience heralded the arrival on stage of the pianist who minced towards Adrian as the latter rose uncertainly and shook hands.

Adrian turned to the audience. Perspiration poured down his face but his throat was dry. He spoke in a muffled croak.

"Ladies and gentlemen. I need hardly say what a great honour it is to welcome our illustrious and distinguished guest, none other than madam er…. er… madam……."

"I`m a bloke if you don`t mind," hissed the pianist, as the audience froze.

"Of course, of course," Adrian stammered, hastily putting on an indulgent smile. "It is my great pleasure to welcome Mr er….er… Mr Mystery who has come all the way from er… er… overseas to entertain us with what I am sure will be a remarkable rendition of er… er… a piece of music known and appreciated by us all."

As the audience clapped enthusiastically, Adrian retreated and hastily handed a note to a passing usher. "Indisposed. You do the bloody vote of thanks. But find out first who the bugger is."

AND NOW THE FUTURE

Rosemary entered Madam Foresight`s tent just for a giggle.

The fortune-teller was sitting in semi-darkness behind a table on which was placed a crystal ball. Her hair was blonde though it could have been a wig. It was partly covered by a red scarf and the rest of her was concealed by a large shawl. She stared at her visitor though eyes that were small and green. Penetrating, Rosemary said to herself, that`s the word. She waited for the sound of a mysterious cracked voice.

The voice was entirely normal. The woman couldn`t have been more than 25 or 30.

"Show me your hands."

Rosemary obediently placed her hands on the table. If only she had managed to wash them after eating candy floss at the fair! What an embarrassment if the resulting stickiness distorted her entire future.

There was a long silence. Rosemary wondered whether the strange figure on the other side of the table had drifted off to sleep. She coughed nervously. This seemed to trigger the fortune-teller into action.

"I can see tragedy in your life when you were quite young. You were distraught for a long time."

Rosemary's mind shot back to her entirely happy childhood. Then she remembered how upset she had been when her hamster, Bertie, had died. She nodded encouragingly.

"But something good emerged. You established a relationship which opened new doors for you."

Rosemary cast her mind back once more. After Bertie's departure her parents had kindly bought her a puppy, imaginatively called Bertrand. She had spent long hours attempting to train him to open and shut the front door with his nose. It seemed a bit far-fetched but perhaps this was what Madam Foresight had in mind. Rosemary nodded again, though more doubtfully.

The fortune-teller gave the crystal ball a quick tweak. "I can see disturbance, even violence."

Good Heavens, thought Rosemary. That must be the Maltese flame-thrower. I had almost forgotten about him. "Could I ask about the future, please?" she inquired cautiously.

Madam Foresight showed signs of irritation. "I'm coming to that. I can only see into the future when I have understood the past."

Rosemary, suitably chastened, waited for more.

"You are not married but I see someone who may be a partner. You live in a small house with a garden. I see a large garden."

Getting warmer, Rosemary conceded, but it could all be guess-work.

"You work but you do not feel fulfilled."

Nice one, but what next?

"You are going to change your life-style soon. I can see young people, yes, children around you. You are going to live a long time. You have nothing to fear but soon you may have an unhappy experience. You will recover quickly and go from strength to strength. That is all."

"Thank you," Rosemary said, getting up. What a fraud! I`ve a good mind to ask for my money back. I could have done better myself.

She stepped briskly out of the tent, caught her foot on a length of rope, and fell awkwardly. There was a sharp crack as her ankle gave way.

Just as well I didn`t ask for my money back, Rosemary reflected at the hospital as she waited to be processed. This was an unhappy experience all right.

"Name and occupation?" asked the bored nurse-receptionist at the desk when Rosemary`s turn came.

"Rosemary Slidehill, otherwise known as Madam Crystal, fortune-teller. And in answer to your next questions, I am about to marry my partner who is a full-time gardener with 3 children. I am going to live a long time and I intend to go from strength to strength."

The receptionist looked up, suddenly interested . "A fortune-teller! Did you foresee that you were going to have this accident?"

"No," Rosemary admitted, "but I rather think I know someone who did."

A NIGHT AT THE OPERA

SYNOPSIS

Act One

<u>The curtain rises</u>. The scene is a forest glade dominated by the boughs of a large tree.

Princess Kakoffony is hanging upside down from a bird`s nest. She sings the haunting aria *Oshito, ke eest mes bloomerkrutchons distortos*? ("Oh dear, why are my knickers in a twist?")

But help is at hand. The Three Women of Doubtful Virtue, Flossiva, Whipsolitcha, and Brothola, arrive dressed as mountain goats. They gasp for some minutes at the sight of the hapless Princess. Then, with the aid of a convenient rope ladder, Flossiva climbs towards the nest and with a practised hand rips off the outer clothing of the Princess to reveal a mermaid`s tail. As the Princess, now freed, descends the ladder, she sings *Oona notte grass te suffiko* ("I cannot thank you enough"), and is joined by a choir of elderly cardinals who arrive on roller skates.

The mood becomes sombre. Lucinda, betrothed to Pedroitus the fisherman, suspects the latter of infidelity with the Princess. *Pusco mis te rodus hut notte strahert* ("Promise me your rod has not wandered") she sings. "Fear not," Pedroitus replies, "my rod is safe in your hands". The cardinals nod sagely and intone a brief descant *Oost veruca* ("That is true"). But Lucinda still entertains her suspicions and in order to test Pedroitus`s love for her, she seizes a garden fork. *Whit te gong fare mut ko gitten implemento* ("What are you going to do with that garden fork?") he cries.

At that moment, Fabula, an itinerant psychotherapist, enters pushing an empty pram. She offers assistance. *Ke hist te notte fidoca*? ("Why have you no faith?") Before Lucinda can reply, the Princess herself intervenes. *Sif te inditto hit, te inditto mis* ("If you accuse him, you accuse me.") The cardinals see the force of this and together they chant *Oost veruca.*

"Why do you believe Pedroitus loves me?" the Princess persists. "Because I know he loves fish and you have a mermaid`s tail," Lucinda retorts.

Now Fabula`s wisdom comes to the rescue. "That does not follow," she declares and so sings *Permesse tros spookas judgementos* ("Let the gods decide.") "I can hear rain coming," she continues, "and should there be a clap of thunder then the good name and fidelity of Pedroitus and the Princess shall stand for ever unsullied." The cardinals, once more impressed, sing *Oost veruca*.

There is a long silence. Tension mounts, to be followed by a deafening clap of thunder.

Lucinda throws away the garden fork and embraces Pedroitus as she sings *Ke oona te dubitante*? ("Why did I doubt you?") The Princess in turn embraces Lucinda. They depart with the cardinals and all process behind Fabula as she wheels her pram into the distance. Only the Three Women of Doubtful Virtue remain. They stand to one side, their horns interlocking. Together they sing *Grass tes ospookas fir ko indispensable bombardo di furiosbum.* ("Thank you, oh gods, for that most helpful clap of thunder.")

<u>The curtain falls</u>

~~~~~~~~~~~~~~~~

INTERVAL

~~~~~~~~~~~~~~~~

There will be an interval of 1 hour 15 minutes. To avoid the possibility of a crush at the crush bar, our patrons are strongly advised to order refreshments, particularly champagne, caviar, and smoked salmon, beforehand. CD`s of many old and all-too-forgettable productions in this theatre are available in the foyer. A bell closely resembling a fire-alarm will be sounded repeatedly and unnecessarily early. For the convenience of those patrons who are in their place when the curtain rises, patrons who are not seated will remain unseated.

Act Two

The curtain rises. The scene is the garden of Princess Kakoffony`s residence. The Princess, ensconced in a gazebo, is engaged in her toiletry, assisted by her hand-maiden Seekofanti.

"Five years have passed," the Princess declares, "and I have achieved nothing."

"But you married the Baron and gave birth to a beautiful duck," Seekofanti points out.

"*Oost veruca*," the Princess agrees, " but my husband suspects that he is not the father."

Ovacuoso suspectrum ("Oh what a baseless suspicion") the hand-maiden sings. "Whom does he suspect?"

"He suspects Pedroitus the fisherman."

The elderly cardinals now enter on motorised zimmer-frames and scoot effortlessly round the stage singing *Oost crapeetus* ("That is nonsense"). "Why does your husband so suspect?" the oldest cardinal inquires, bringing his zimmer-frame to a halt.

"Because my child is a duck and my husband is a man."

Fabula enters, pulling a cart loaded with hay. "But you have a mermaid`s tail," she points out. "That assuredly could make a difference."

Oona notte misleedos te ("I cannot deceive you") the Princess sobs. "Once I loved Pedroitus."

The cardinals are shocked. "You cannot have done so. *Tros spookas sot judgementoried.*" ("The gods so decided").

The Princess continues to sob. "Sometimes the gods get it wrong."

The cardinals are outraged. *Oost crapeetus*, they exclaim. "What is the point of having gods if they get things wrong?"

Fabula pours oil upon troubled waters by distributing her bales of hay. *Whit hut pisto hut pisto* ("What has passed has passed") she observes sagely. And then to the cardinals, she says "Trust me. Throw away your zimmer-frames. You have no need of them. *Ke hist te notte fidoca*?"

The cardinals hesitate and then, one by one, they cast aside their zimmer-frames. Each of the cardinals slowly topples over and falls to the ground.

A lone trumpet heralds the arrival of the Baron, fresh from the hunting field. He enters, a dead ostrich slung lightly over his shoulders.

Whit ist ki catastrobom? ("What is the problem?") he asks the Princess.

"Sire, I know you believe that Pedroitus is the father of our duck".

The Baron is silent.

Fabula again intervenes. "Sire, Does the duck not look more like a hunter than a fisherman?"

The cardinals rise to their feet and gleefully seize their zimmer-frames. *Oost veruca*, they chant as they re-load the bales of hay onto the cart.

"You are right," the Baron concedes. He takes the Princess in his arms. *Ke oona te dubitante*? Symbolically, she seizes a garden rake and so lifts the ostrich from his shoulders and places it on top of the hay.

All leave joyfully except Seekofanti and Fabula.

Seekofanti says, *Te eest ut celestaria* ("You are a star"). Fabula collects the last bales of hay. As she pulls the now heavily laden cart, she sings *Ustoos addito at verto keet bonkenshaften* ("There is more to life than making love").

<u>The curtain falls (and is caught by a passing stage-hand)</u>

PRIVATE LIVES

The balcony of the Greek hotel bedroom had a charming view of the distant sea. But it was spoilt because of the half-hearted little walls which divided the balcony into four. If the neighbours came out onto their section of the balcony, you could say goodbye to privacy. At least, that was how Ronald regarded it as he stood admiring the evening view whilst his wife battled inside with the bathroom shower.

Immediately to his left, a pleasant elderly German couple were enjoying a quiet drink. Ronald leant over the little wall. "Hallo there, you`re German, aren`t you?"

"That is correct."

"My father fought in the War, you know. He called you lot the Huns of course. He managed to kill quite a few of you, apparently. And he was proud of it, I can tell you."

The couple exchanged glances, and without a word picked up their drinks and retreated to the safety of their bedroom.

Ronald turned his attention to the middle-aged French husband and wife who were sitting to his right reading their magazines. "Hallo, you`re French, aren`t you?"

"Oui, M`sieur, et vous?"

"I don`t speak a word of your language, I`m glad to say. It beats me why everyone doesn`t speak English. We call you Frogs, as you probably know. Do you understand what I`m saying?"

The French couple stood up. "All too well, M`sieur." They went inside.

At that moment, a young Englishman wearing only a pair of shorts came out onto his part of the balcony.

"Hallo, you`re English, aren`t you? I believe you`re on your honeymoon."

The young man almost blushed. "Yes, I am as a matter of fact."

"Had a good screw, have you then?"

The man gave a squawk of dismay and rushed back through the door.

Ronald called out to his wife. "You can come onto the balcony now if you like, dear. I can`t think why but we seem to have got it all to ourselves."

A CERTAIN AGE

She was only fourteen years old but she was causing havoc with Colin`s emotions. It wasn`t her fault. The snag was that he was aged fifty-two and he was happily married with a teenage daughter of his own.

It had all started when Hannah, their sixteen-year old, had said, "Would it be all right if I have a friend to stay for Easter? Her Mum and Dad are away somewhere. She`s called Katie and she`s cool."

Colin and Molly glanced at each other and nodded. "Yes, of course, but she will have to sleep in the attic because there`s no other room," Molly said. "When do you think she will want to come?"

"Tomorrow afternoon," Hannah said. "I`ve invited her. I was sure you wouldn`t mind."

When Colin got home tired from work the next day he had forgotten all about the arrival of Katie. Hannah introduced her briefly but he was relieved when after a couple of minutes they both went upstairs. No need to get involved in polite conversation.

Next morning, however, when he was in the kitchen making a quick cup of coffee, the door opened and she came in. She was tall for her age, with long blonde hair, and was wearing blue jeans and a tight T-shirt. She had bare feet.

She hesitated uncertainly. "Oh, sorry. I didn`t know there was anyone in here. Is it all right if I . . . ?"

"Dear me, yes! Come in. Help yourself to anything you want. I don`t suppose that Hannah is up yet?"

"No, it`s a bit early in the morning for her." She gave him a broad grin and his heart gave a sudden thump. What a gorgeous girl, he thought, making a conscious effort to take his eyes off her. "I am off to work now," he said, in a matter-of-fact voice, "but Molly should be down soon and no doubt Hannah will put in an appearance when she feels the urge." They smiled at each other. He walked out of the kitchen in a daze. In the space of a few seconds, his life had been turned over.

On the way to work, he could think about nothing else. Was she really only fourteen? How long had Hannah known her? Who and where were her mum and dad? At the office, he remained so distracted that even his boss, who rarely noticed anything apart from profit margins, commented. "What`s up, Colin? Trouble at home?"

"Dear me, no," Colin replied, "But I would like to take an extra day off over Easter."

He could hardly wait to get home that evening. When he did, he was bitterly disappointed to discover that the girls had gone out on some expedition and would not be back until late.

"It's rather a relief to have a quiet evening to ourselves, isn't it?" Molly said comfortingly. "And there is a repeat of an Inspector Morse story on television. Put your feet up and we can have supper as we watch."

But for once, the murder investigations of Inspector Morse failed to hold Colin's attention. He thought about his brief conversation with Katie that morning and at the way they had smiled together, as though sharing a secret. *And* she was going to stay for a whole week!

During the following days, Colin remained in a complete state. He wanted to spend all the time he could with Katie and he felt childishly resentful when she and Hannah went off to visit other friends. At the same time, he told himself over and over again that the whole thing was absurd. He was old enough to be her father or even grandfather, she clearly didn't feel the same way about him as he did about her, and anyway there was no reason to suppose that when she became sixteen she would be willing to marry him or live with him, quite apart from any problems that Molly might understandably create.

When Easter came to an end and Katie departed, life started to resume its normal course. But Colin still found himself thinking about her time and time again though he felt guilty and disloyal towards the ever-kind Molly who looked quizzically at him on occasions but made no comment.

When Whitsun was approaching, Colin asked Hannah over breakfast in a casual tone of voice, "Is that nice friend of yours, what's her name, Katie, coming to stay with us again?"

"No, she is going to be with her Mum and Dad."

Colin lifted the newspaper to hide his expression.

"But," Hannah continued, "would it be okay for her to spend three nights with us in the cottage in the last week of July? She might overlap with my other friend Stephanie but that would only be for one night."

Colin's throat went dry. He almost dropped the newspaper. "Dear me," he said, "I will have a word with Mummy but I'm sure it will be all right."

They always rented the same cottage by the sea in Norfolk. For Colin, the next few weeks passed in a haze of anticipation. Then at last the holiday came and they reached the cottage. The following day Katie arrived. She had had her hair tinted and somehow looked a bit older. She greeted Colin warmly and he gave her a kiss on one cheek.

"Shall we all go swimming tomorrow?" he suggested during the evening meal in the cramped kitchen. "It will be a bit cold but it should be bearable." There was general agreement.

Next day the sun was shining. "We will go ahead," Hannah and Katie announced. Colin and Molly followed them down to the sea a few minutes later. The two girls were splashing about happily. Katie was wearing a two-piece. She waved. "Come on in. It`s great!"

Colin looked at her appraisingly as he got closer. Then he stopped in his tracks so suddenly that Molly almost tripped over him.

Katie had got a ring through her navel. It`s revolting, Colin thought, absolutely revolting. I can`t bear those things. What on earth makes people wear them? Ugh!

Now he saw her in an entirely different light. The dream had shattered. She was only a school-girl, nice enough but obviously silly. How could he ever have thought that there was more to her than that?

He was irritable and subdued for the rest of the day and the following day as well. Eventually, when they were alone, Molly said, "What`s the matter?"

He couldn`t bear the situation any longer. He told her. He ended up, "I know I have been so stupid. A fourteen-year old girl! It`s ridiculous. I don`t imagine you will ever be able to understand."

Molly looked away into the distance. "As a matter of fact, I do understand. I went through the same thing last year. Do you remember that nice young boy who Hannah brought to stay with us a few times?"

Colin gave a cry of disbelief. "But for Heaven`s sake, he was only thirteen!"

"I know," Molly said rather sadly. "But he looked much older. It's all right. Nothing happened but for a few months I was besotted. Then it fizzled out."

"Why was that?" Colin inquired cautiously.

"It was his feet," Molly explained simply. "One day he was wearing sandals. I saw his toes. They looked like talons. That was the end."

There was silence for a few moments. "I suppose it's all to do with us reaching what people call *a certain age*," Colin said slowly.

There was a shout of delight outside. The door opened. Hannah swept in ahead of a tall dark-haired girl. "Mummy! Daddy! This is Stephanie, but you can call her Steph."

Stephanie came in, flicking her hair back over one shoulder. She had large brown eyes and gave a warm, confident smile.

Colin felt as though he had been stabbed in the groin. Oh dear me! he thought. I must still be at *a certain age*. Here we go again!

A FLIGHT OF FANCY

In his own view at least, Marcus was a very important businessman. So naturally he was travelling Business Class on the flight to Prague.

As he settled comfortably into his seat and accepted a glass of champagne from the brittle air-stewardess, he thought how admirably the arrangements had been made by Liz, his highly efficient secretary. She had insisted on seeing him off at Heathrow. This was her last day with him before she returned to her native Australia. She had been an excellent secretary, he reflected, even if she had been a bit stroppy about her salary. And what a nice smile she had given him as they parted!

He took out his lap-top, not because he needed it, but in order to impress other passengers. He noticed, with slight irritation, that apart from those who were studying *The Financial Times*, most of them were already balancing lap-tops on their knees.

After an uninspiring light meal, (salad, cold chicken and apple tart), "Even worse than Economy," he commented to the passenger sitting beside him, he took out the documents in his brief-case and studied the contract that he was due to sign in a couple of hours` time. All the details had been agreed. Apart from the tight deadline, nothing could go wrong.

When he returned to London that evening, he would be richer by nearly a quarter of a million pounds. He gave a sigh of satisfaction at the thought. True, tax would have to come out of this but even so there should be more than enough to buy the new BMW which he had set his heart on, and enough even to satisfy the insatiable financial demands of his present wife. His accountant could be trusted to juggle the figures so that neither of his ex- wives would find out about the transaction. Heaven knows, he deserved a reward after all the work he had put into this project.

The pilot`s voice crackled above his head with an incomprehensible announcement in which only the word "Prague" could be heard. The `plane was clearly on its descent.

Marcus had a final look at the documents in his hand. No! "Fuck!" he exclaimed loudly, to the surprise of the neighbouring passenger who looked inquiringly at him.

"I shouldn`t be on this `plane at all. I have a very important meeting in just over an hour`s time but it`s in Paris, not Prague."

The passenger glanced, unnecessarily, at his watch. "Then you`ll never make it. How on earth did that happen?"

Marcus almost choked. "I don`t know. My secretary made all the arrangements. She`s very efficient. She`s…………."

His voice tailed away. He remembered the smile she had given him at the airport. It had seemed such a nice innocent smile at the time.

Now he understood. "Oh, fuck!" he said again.

But his neighbour had lost interest, and already was toying with the seat-belt.

Neither of them could know that in a few moments a bomb in the aircraft's hold would blow up. There were to be no survivors.

When Liz learnt about this at her brother's ranch in Australia she was quite upset. "I blame myself," she told two surprised-looking cows. "He was a mean bastard but I wish now I hadn't put him on that flight. Fuck!"

HOLIDAY OF A LIFETIME

Sam wriggled his bottom further into the deck-chair and immediately regretted it. The faint movement had been sufficient to attract his wife`s attention in the adjacent chair.

"Will you stop doing that? You are always twitching."

Only at the sound of your voice, Sam muttered to himself. But aloud he said in the remote tone he had learnt to adopt over the years, "Sorry, Thelma. Do you want to go for a walk along the beach?"

"No, not with all those kids running up and down shouting and screaming and making a nuisance of themselves. They`ve no respect for folk like me who just want a bit of peace and quiet. And if I do go for a walk, I don`t want you coming with me, thank you very much." Ostentatiously she moved her chair a few feet further away and returned to her magazine.

Sam studied her from behind the safety of his sun-glasses. He asked himself, as he had done a hundred times before, what had possessed him to marry her in the first place. That was twelve years ago. Within weeks, Thelma had stormed out and gone to live with her mother, a spiteful little woman with bad breath, and her father who bore a striking physical resemblance to Adolf Hitler. Unhappily, Thelma had soon quarrelled with her mother and had returned to live with Sam. They had no children, and divorce would have been a simple solution. On the other hand, neither of them had found anyone else and, with the aid of apathy, the marriage just about survived.

Sam closed his eyes. The sound of the sea mingled pleasantly enough with the noise of children laughing and playing and mobile-phones ringing. In a couple of hours, Sam reflected, he and Thelma would stroll back to the third-rate boarding-house where they stayed every year and would have an indifferent meal in the cramped dining-room which smelt of cats. Afterwards they would sit gazing vacantly at the small television set in the so-called TV lounge. Then Thelma would give a huge unsmothered yawn and would announce that she was bored and was going to bed but that there was no need for him to come up until she had got off to sleep which Heaven Alone knew she deserved, thank you very much. Any attempt by Sam to vary this routine would be met by antagonistic grunts, possibly accompanied by references to his obvious lack of consideration for her and his failure to understand that it was her holiday as much as his and that if she didn`t want to go out or do anything it was not for him to complain. And if he was thinking about going out for a drink by himself, he could forget it. She hadn`t come on holiday so that he could just go sloping off by himself, thank you very much.

Sam woke up with a start. He could see from his watch that he must have dozed off for at least half-an-hour. He glanced cautiously towards the deck-chair nearby. It was empty. Sam sighed with relief. A reprieve!

Ten minutes went by. Twenty. Thirty. After an hour, Sam was conscious of a variety of conflicting emotions: pleasure, relief, concern, surprise. Thelma would occasionally wander off by herself along the cliff-top but rarely for more than twenty minutes. Sam extricated himself from his chair and walked along the parade, then to the cliff-top, and back again. Still no sign of her. Her magazine and shopping bag remained underneath her chair. Sam picked them up and walked slowly towards the boarding-house. There was no sign of her there.

At nine o`clock that evening, he reported her disappearance to the police station. On the way back to the boarding-house, he felt the urge for a drink and turned in to *The Laughing Soldier* for a half pint of bitter. Soon he was chatting with the friendly barmaid. After another drink or two, he told the story of his missing wife to a receptive and increasingly animated crowd. At closing-time, he staggered guiltily back to the boarding-house, expecting that somehow Thelma would have returned and been in a suitable rage about his sustained disregard for her welfare. But there was only a note which had been pushed under his door to say that there was still no news. He didn`t know whether to laugh or cry. The trouble was that he`d had one of the best evenings he could remember having for years.

He called into the police station at ten o`clock the next morning as arranged. He thought it was just a matter of routine and that there would be nothing to report. But there was!

The fatherly sergeant asked him to go into a small room. "I`m sorry, sir, it`s bad news. Are you prepared for the worst?"

Sam nodded.

"I don`t think there can be much doubt about it. It`s your wife. Her body was washed up on the shore two hours ago. It looks as though she must have fallen from the cliff. I`m very sorry. Would you mind coming to the mortuary to identify the body?"

Sam nodded again. Suddenly he began to shake convulsively. Tears of laughter coursed down his cheeks. He buried his face in his hands. The policeman looked away, embarrassed. "I`ll get you a cup of tea," he said. To his colleagues outside, he confided, "Poor sod! He is taking it very badly."

It was the same at the mortuary. Sam was overcome with mirth. The body was Thelma`s all right, there could be no mistaking it. Tears of laughter poured down. Even the mortuary assistant was sympathetic. He had rarely seen a man so distressed.

Later that day, Sam sat in his familiar deck-chair, a marvellous single chair, with not another within thirty feet. He closed his eyes, pondering over the events of the last twenty-four hours. That evening, he decided, he would go out on the town and then he would visit *The Laughing Soldier* again and chat up the barmaid and get everyone to buy him drinks to console him for the loss of his wife.

He gave a contented sigh. Of course, he could not speak for her but for him this was turning out to be a marvellous holiday. In fact, the holiday of a lifetime.

BRASS NECK

Edward studied his patient carefully. "Good to see you again, but you missed your last appointment with me. Why was that?"

Stephen looked down at his shoes. "I can't remember."

"Was it anything to do with your Urges?"

Stephen raised his head and glanced reluctantly at the psychiatrist. "It might have been."

"Are you still visiting the zoo? Just before dark?"

"Yes."

"And it's still the giraffes that you are interested in?"

"Yes."

"We have talked about this before but I want you to tell me precisely what the attraction is."

"It's their necks."

"Of course I understand that, and we both know what you did to your grandmother when you were a teenager. But that was nearly ten years ago. So what is in your mind when you look at the giraffes?"

"You're the psychiatrist. You should know."

"Stephen! This is not helpful. A few months ago it was swans. You explained why you were attracted towards them. But for me to go on treating you, you have got to tell me what you are thinking about when you are looking at the giraffes."

Stephen averted his eyes. After a pause: "I think about my grandmother."

"I thought so, but that was all a long time ago. And, as you know, she`s no longer with us. Don`t you think the stage has come to put that behind you?"

"I can`t. That`s why I have to go to the zoo. I was there last night."

Edward sighed. "Well, there are various ways we can go on dealing with the er…. problem. One is to increase the amount of your medication. Another is to………Stephen, why are you coming towards me like that? Stephen, for God`s sake, what are you doing? Help! Help!"

But it was too late. Stephen kept both hands round Edward`s neck until there were no longer signs of life. "Sorry, doc. I ought not to have done that to you. But you never really did understand my Urges."

At that moment the telephone on the desk rang twice. Stephen cautiously picked it up.

The receptionist, unaware of the drama which had just taken place, spoke quietly. "Doctor, is your patient still with you? There are two police officers here to see him. It`s about some unpleasantness at the zoo. Three giraffes have had it in the neck. Murdered! I`ve told the police I`m sure it can`t have anything to do with the patient. Shall I show them in now?"

LESSONS

"Toe tiffy tum boo hoo, and *not* tiffy tum hoo toe boo. And what are you doing with that finger?"

Giles` method of teaching the piano was a touch out of date as well as being a constant source of irritation to his pupils, young and old.

He was sitting beside Louisa, aged twelve, who with her lips slightly parted and with great concentration was carefully murdering one of Chopin`s simpler works.

She took the hint and moved the offending finger on to a black key before resuming her homicidal activities.

Meanwhile Giles was studying her breasts which, despite her youth, were already making conspicuous progress. Fortunately, he reflected, he was not interested in boys. In fact they irritated him with their tiresome obsessions about computers and sport. But girls were different in more ways than one. He wondered briefly whether a small alteration to his present advert for music teachers in the Yellow Pages - *Giles strikes the right chord : the Young especially welcome* - might result in an increased supply of daughters being entrusted to him. And what a wise decision he had made years ago to allow his membership of the Society of

Musicians to lapse! Now he wasn't on a register from which he could be struck off.

His reverie was interrupted by a peculiarly horrific discord and his pupil bursting into tears. "It's no good," she sobbed, searching for a handkerchief. "I'm never going to manage this piece."

"Of course you will," Giles said, taking the opportunity to put one arm round her shoulders. "Let's take it slowly, one bar at a time." He switched on what he imagined was a reassuring smile though it emerged more like a leer. "You're doing fine. In fact," he lied, "you're one of my most talented pupils."   Reluctantly he removed his arm and the lesson continued without incident, or at least none that Louisa was aware of.

But when she got up to leave she announced without warning, "Sorry, I forgot to tell you last time. I can't have any more lessons with you. As Dad has gone off with someone, my Mum and me are emigrating to Canada next week."

Giles was stunned. Yet another of his diminishing group of pupils lost for ever, quite apart from the obvious physical attractions of this one.

All he could do was to stammer, "Oh dear! Boo hoo."

~~~~~~~~~~

Three months later he bumped into her in the street. "Hallo!" he said, astonished. "I thought you had gone to Canada."

Louisa didn`t look him in the eye. "No, `twasn`t true. My Mum told me to tell you that. We still live here."

"But what about your piano lessons? Have you given them up?"

Louisa went red. "No. I have them at home now. Julie, she`s the cow who`s moved in with Mum, gives me them. But I hate them, I really hate them. She keeps on, well, you know, looking at me and touching me and that stuff."

Unexpectedly Louisa glanced up and smiled shyly at Giles. "I wish you were still teaching me. I always felt so safe with you."

KEEPING WATCH

Sarah reckoned there was much to be said for being a store detective.

"I`ve got a nose for them shop-lifters," she would tell her friends. "It`s just a matter of keeping watch. I can look round the store, right?, and straightaway I can sus out if there`s something dodgy, d`you know what I mean? They comes in all shapes and sizes. Fat and thin, some tarted up like there`s no tomorrow, some look like they`ve just fallen out of bed, old and young, the lot. You can`t trust nobody."

Today, dressed for her job in the plainest of plain clothes, and clutching a carrier bag in one hand and a wire basket in the other, she was unobtrusively watching a couple of teenage girls. There was just something about them, the way they kept together, the way they kept on looking around, they must be up to no good. Sarah glanced at her watch. Nearly three o`clock and almost time to go off duty so she could pick up the kids from school. The sooner these girls did or didn`t do something the better.

The two teenagers went to the check-out. They hadn`t put anything in their pockets as far as Sarah could see, and they paid for the few items they had in their basket. The alarm didn`t ring as they went out through the door. Okay so perhaps they had just been doing a practice run or something. Sarah was not prepared to admit even to herself that she might be wrong.

"Will you come to the manager's office, please?"

She looked up. Ben, the tall uniformed security man was standing beside her.

"What do you mean, come to the manager's office?"

"I've been watching you the last ten minutes and I figure you're up to no good."

"Don't be stupid. I'm the store detective, right?"

Ben showed no sign of recognising her. "You can try explaining that in the manager's office."

Together they walked in silence through the store and into the office, which was deserted.

Ben closed the door. He and Sarah kissed. "Well, Babe, what have you managed to get this time?" he asked.

Sarah proudly opened her carrier bag. "I've got these gloves for you and a scarf for meself, and I've got these things for the kids and a bit of food for our supper like. How've you done?"

Ben took off a brand new leather belt and removed a couple of DVDs from a side pocket in his jacket. "Here, you take these and I'll let you out of the back door. You'd best be off now. Be good." He gave her a wink.

"And you. See you later."

After he left the office, Ben went back into the main store to stand, impressively, near the check-outs.

The cocky young trainee manager came up to him a few minutes later. "Hi! Ben. Seen any villains today?"

"No, but don`t you worry. It`s just a matter of keeping watch. Trust me, I know what I am doing."

"I`m sure you do, but you`d better come with me. There`s a police officer waiting for you. As you`re a security man, I`m surprised you didn`t spot the little camera in the office ceiling. After all, it`s just a matter of keeping watch."

THE BARE TRUTH

She had never undressed a man before and she was sick with excitement.

He stood in front of her, half-smiling, his arms raised.

She began to undo the buttons of his soft, smooth white shirt. Her hands were shaking and her heart was pounding as though she had been running a marathon. The first two buttons came away without difficulty but the next was a real struggle. Somehow it didn`t seem right to apologise. Fortunately the next few buttons were easier. Now they were all undone. She lifted the shirt over his shoulders and carelessly threw it onto a chair. He wasn`t wearing a vest.

What was the etiquette now? He was still silent and made no move to help, though she fancied she detected a gleam of some strong emotion in his eyes.

Slowly she undid his belt and, looking away with an odd sense of embarrassment, she undid the zip and let his trousers fall to the ground. He had been in bare feet since the beginning and now he was naked apart from a thong.

Her embarrassment disappeared and with a quick movement she slipped the thong down to his feet.

Disappointingly, unlike her, he showed no signs of excitement. But in a strange way he was good to look at.

"Darling man, you are beautiful," she whispered, and leant down to kiss him.

At that moment the store-room door burst open and two other girl shop-assistants charged in. They stopped, astonished, and then shrieked with laughter.

"So that`s what you`ve been getting up to! We thought you just came in here for a quick drag."

She went scarlet in the face.

"I was only trying to get some clothes for a customer," she explained unconvincingly.

"Yeah, pull the other one," the girls said, clutching each other helplessly.

If the dummy had had a brain in his head he might have joined in the laughter. But as it was, he just stood there with his fixed half-smile.

THE POOL

At the age of nineteen, Eleanor had discovered the pleasures of skinny dipping. But only if no one else was around. Her parents and friends were stuffy about that sort of thing and her younger brother had reached the age of making coarse remarks.

Fortunately there was an idyllic pool only a short distance from her home. In the far distance lay an old abbey but the pool was surrounded by tall trees and bushes and was almost completely hidden from the outside world. A few local people would sometimes walk their dogs nearby but never, so far as Eleanor knew, in mid-afternoon. And today the sun was blazing hot and the water was warm and clean.

So she swam gently beyond the reeds, enjoying the sensual caress of the water around her limbs. Then she lay on her back, paddling gently. She was having a great time. And yet somehow there was a sense of dissatisfaction. What am I doing with my life? she asked herself. What`s it all about? I just seem to be floating aimlessly along.

Suddenly her reverie was interrupted. A distinct shiver ran along her bare spine. She was being watched. She had no doubt about it. She raised her head and looked discreetly from right to left. Nothing stirred. Could it be just imagination? No, she was quite certain. The bushes were thick and a peeping tom could easily be crouching behind them out of sight.

Cautiously she swam to the side of the pool where she had put her towel and clothes. She seized the towel, wrapped it round herself, and clambered out of the water. Still no sign of anyone. But she wasn`t going to take any more chances. She dressed quickly and hurried off to the safety of her home.

High up in the abbey, the Abbess sighed and put down her binoculars, the ones she used for "bird-watching" as she occasionally explained. Life was so frustrating at times. That girl had a lovely figure. Those breasts! Those legs! Anyway, it was nearly time for communal prayers.

With her head bent reverently, she prayed for her own soul and for the souls of the other Sisters, and she prayed for forgiveness for her sins. Not, she reasoned, that there was anything much wrong with her having looked at that girl from such a distance, but all the same the Good Lord would probably not have approved. She prayed also that her vibrator - an imaginative gift from a laid-back niece (and which, unlike other gifts, she had understandably decided not to share) - would start functioning again, but once more she recognised that this was probably hoping for too much from the Almighty.

A small miracle was, however, about to occur. For when she later retired to the hard bed in her cell-like room and rummaged about in a battered cardboard box, within seconds the vibrator started its familiar whirr.

The Sister in the adjacent room covered her ears. She had long ceased to believe the Abbess`s story that the sound was that of an electric toothbrush. Who did the Abbess think she was kidding, for God`s sake?

Lying in her comfortable bed at home, Eleanor continued to ponder on her dissatisfaction with life. Suddenly she had a revelation. I have the calling, she whispered to herself. I want to be a nun. I will free myself from all mortal temptations. I will become a novice in that beautiful abbey.

A few weeks later the Abbess recognised Eleanor the moment she entered the abbey although now she was demurely dressed. The Abbess was thrilled to bits. Another miracle! "Praise be to God," she observed to the Sisters. "He moves in a mysterious way all right. Now, would anyone like to borrow my binoculars? I don`t think I`ll need them for a while."

Alice, one of the younger Sisters, raised a hand. "Oh, yes please."

"And what would you be wanting them for?"

"Oh, just for bird-watching."

The other Sisters looked enigmatically at each other. Yes, in relation to Alice, it could be true.

Weeks went by. Summer merged into Autumn. Apart from the rather embarrassing interest that the Abbess took in her, Eleanor adapted well enough to the routine of the abbey. But then everything went pear-shaped, and it was partly because of the pool.

As Eleanor was passing Alice`s room one day, Alice called out, "Quickly! Come and look at this." Alice was standing at the window, peering through the binoculars. Her face was flushed. Eleanor seized the powerful binoculars and trained them on the pool.

Three boys, almost men, were cavorting naked in the water. She knew one of them. It was her brother. He was of no physical interest to her but the others, they were marvellous, they were fantastic, fantastic, fantastic. Her heart rate soared and her mouth went dry. She was overwhelmed by desire. She wanted to be in the pool with them, swimming beside them, and they could stroke her body and she theirs and she would feel the warmth of their bodies against her and, and, and…….

She handed the binoculars back to Alice and buried her head in her hands. "I can`t manage this life any longer. I thought I had the calling but I don`t have. I must get out of here."

The Abbess had seen this coming and was very understanding about it when Eleanor broke the news, even if she did shed a few silent tears in the privacy of her room.

The day after Eleanor had left, the Abbess sat pensively at the head of the long refectory table. Life was going to feel empty once more, apart of course from the spiritual side, and matters weren't helped by that God-forsaken vibrator having packed up again. Then she had a cheering thought.

"Sister Alice," she called out. "May I have my binoculars back, please?"

Under the rules of the abbey, only the Abbess was allowed to speak at meal-times. So Alice simply bowed her head in silent, dismayed agreement.

This time no explanation was given. And none was needed.

CLASS WARFARE

Mr Brown looked at his Latin class of teenage boys with dislike.

If parents were stupid enough to chuck away vast fortunes on having their sons educated in Latin, Greek and other weird subjects, that was their look-out. But the whole thing was quite pointless. The little bastards spent all their time day-dreaming about sex and computer games. The Classics could get lost!

The boy Jackson in the back row was obviously not concentrating, at least not on the Latin text in front of him. "Here, YOU," Mr Brown bawled, "How would you translate the words *Ubi caritas et amor, Deus ibi est* ?"

Without a moment's hesitation the reply came, "Where there is affection and love, there God is."

Shit! And I thought I had got him, Mr Brown said to himself. "Very good. May I inquire how you managed to do that immediate translation?"

"It was obvious, sir. What else could it mean?"

Shit! And the whole class was giggling. Round one to Jackson.

At coffee-break in the common-room, Mr Brown told his colleagues what had happened. "The boy's not all that clever. How the hell did he manage to come back with that spot-on translation?"

The rest of the teaching staff shook their heads in suitable bewilderment.

"I could find out for you," the Greek master offered.

"How would you do that?" Mr Brown inquired, unwisely.

"I have my sources."

A frisson ran round the room. The Greek master`s relationship with an angelic-looking boy in the same class as Jackson had become all too well known.

A couple of days later the Greek master smugly supplied the information. "I happen to have found out that your quotation was included in a hymn that was sung by the choir last week. Jackson is in the choir. In fact he usually sits next to-------."

"Yes, yes. I know who you mean. Well, that`s very interesting. So one could hardly say that Jackson was being dishonest. It was more a case of *suppressio veri.*"

"I suppose so. I wonder how one would say that in Greek? Anyway, how are you going to deal with Jackson? My er…. contact tells me that he is getting a bit above himself."

"I will think of something."

The next day Mr Brown entered the classroom with a sense of anticipation. He lost no time.

"Jackson," he said pleasantly enough. "You`re an expert on translation though you may find it a bit difficult this time. These words don`t come straight out of a hymn. How would you translate *blandae mendacia linguae* and *qui desiderat pacem, praeparet bellum*?"

The reply came immediately. "Falsehoods of a smooth tongue, and who desires peace, let him prepare for war. Sir."

Shit! "Very good. May I inquire how you managed to do those immediate translations?"

"It was obvious, sir. What else could they mean?"

Round two to Jackson.

At coffee-break in the common-room, Mr Brown told his colleagues what had happened. "How the hell did that boy manage to come back again with those spot-on translations?"

"I could find out for you," the Greek master offered.

"Oh, you needn't trouble. I rather think I'll have a little chat myself with that good-looking young friend of yours."

Once more, a sudden frisson. And if looks could kill, Mr Brown's expectation of life had just become zilch. The Rubicon had been crossed. The war of the Classic masters had begun.

Back in the classroom, the indomitable Jackson continued to prepare for round three. The lessons in Geography, ("The nomadic tribes of Peru"), History, ("Charles the First: where did I go wrong?"), and Religious Studies, ("Good Lord, whither?"), passed completely over his head. Feverishly he studied the numerous Latin texts hidden under his desk. I will catch up with the lessons later, he told himself. But now it must be Latin, Latin, Latin.

For this was the only way he could achieve his burning ambition: a knock-out blow in round three. How else could he secure the praise and admiration of his class-mates? And above all, of the angelic-looking boy who sat next to him in the choir, the boy he loved?

CHILD`S PLAY

"Well, Emily, tell me how you get on at school. Who`s your best friend?"

Emily hated grown-ups asking that question. It was so paternising, a word she`d picked up a few days ago. She looked down and shuffled her feet.

"Surely you must have one." His voice was amused.

Emily wondered what to say. She could say Jack, who was her really really really best friend but she didn`t feel she could talk about him. Now who else was there?

"Jake," she announced. It was the nearest thing to Jack. As she said it, she knew what would happen. The man she had been told to call Uncle would make fun of her.

"Ho! Ho! Ho! Aren`t you a bit young to have a boyfriend. So who`s Jake?"

"He`s in my class."

"So what`s special about him?"

Emily thought quickly. She would have to invent something. "Well, he`s big and strong and he`s got a nice nose and he laughs a lot. And he shared his crisps with me yesterday."

"You can`t get much more romantic than that."

"What`s *romantic* mean?"

"Sharing your crisps with someone else." This time the amusement in his voice was getting to her.

"I don`t see why I should tell you everything, Uncle. Who`s your best friend?"

"Well, apart from a woman I happen to love, I suppose my best friend is Jeremy."

"Jemmy? What`s special about him, then?"

"Oh, we are real mates. We play golf together every week."

"That sounds boring, boring, boring."

"No, it`s not. It`s fun. Just because you`re mad about swimming, you shouldn`t assume that golf is boring. When you get older, I expect you`ll become more tolerant."

"What`s *tolerant*?"

But at that moment the front door slammed and there was the sound of children`s voices in the hallway.

"Okay," Jack said. "That`s them back. We`d better stop playing this silly game. We`ll never be able to look the kids in the face if they find out what their Mum and Dad get up to."

"Don`t be so paternising," Emily said. They both fell about with laughter.

In the hallway, the children heard the laughter. They looked at each other and then giggled. "They have been playing that silly game again."

ROOM SERVICE

Joanna struggled to cover her ears with the bed-sheet in the stuffy single hotel bedroom. The noise of love-making from the adjacent bedroom was insufferable.

There was a knock at the door. Joanna fumbled for her watch. Eleven pm. "Who is it?" she asked.

"Room service."

"But I haven`t ordered any room service."

"It`s still room service."

Joanna slid out of bed in her nightdress and cautiously opened the door, making sure the chain was in position. She had a restricted view of the man outside. He was the young night-porter she had chatted to briefly earlier in the evening. He was holding a tray with an opened bottle of wine and two glasses.

"Room service," he repeated. "Can I come in?

Joanna opened the door a fraction wider. He was tall, dark-haired and strikingly handsome. But his shirt was half-open and he had a hairy ape-like chest.

"Certainly not!" she said loudly, slamming the door in his face. "Pervert!"

The couple in the bedroom next door had evidently finished their activities and hammered on the wall. "Would you mind making less noise? Some of us are trying to get to sleep."

"You could have fooled me," Joanna shouted back.

She climbed into bed and sat reflecting on the situation. Pity about the hair but that young man had other obvious attractions.

We are all entitled to change our minds, she reasoned to herself. Life as an hotel inspector had its downsides but here was a golden opportunity to test the availability of the night service. Perhaps it might even be regarded as part of her duty.

She picked up the phone. "Room service, please. Wine and two glasses. And hurry."

When she wrote her report later, she dealt very favourably with the quality of the service and the beds.

In fact the hotel was awarded five stars.

THE FACTS OF LIFE

"Mummy! What does *bugger* mean?"

Oh God! Help!

"Where did you hear that word?"

"At school. Someone said I was a silly bugger."

"Then don`t worry. They were just being rude."

"Yes, but what does it mean?"

"I think the best thing is for you to ask Daddy. He should be home soon."

"But I want to know now."

"Well, if you must know, it`s when a man puts his willie up someone`s backside."

"Gosh! Why would anyone want to do that?"

"Some people just seem to like doing it."

"Does Daddy put his willie up your backside?"

"No, certainly not, and anyway that`s not the sort of question you should ask."

"Would Daddy put his willie up my backside?"

"No, of course not. That`s a horrid idea and I rather think it would be illegal."

"Does that mean that if a policeman saw it he would be cross?"

"Yes, almost certainly."

"Are there usually policemen watching it?"

"No, I wouldn`t think so. Hardly ever in fact."

"Why not?"

"I don`t suppose there are enough policemen to go round."

"Why?"

"It`s what the Government would call *lack of resources*."

"What`s that?"

"Not enough money."

"Why don`t they just say so?"

"God knows."

"Does God know everything?"

"Yes."

"Does God do buggers with people?"

"No, certainly not. At least, not directly. Really! What a thought."

"Another boy at school said I was a pain in the arse. Is that the same as doing buggers?"

"No. Yes. No, though now you mention it I suppose they may have something in common. Anyway, I don`t want to go on discussing this. It`s just not nice. Why don`t you go upstairs to your playroom?"

"All right."

She watched him thoughtfully as he ran up the stairs. Had it been a mistake to explain about buggery? He was not very bright, poor boy, but sooner or later someone had to tell him about the facts of life. After all, he was nearly eighteen.

QUESTION TIME IN THE HOUSE OF COMMONS

The Shadow Home Secretary. Is the Home Secretary aware of widespread concern about the low percentage of convictions for rape and what if anything is he proposing to do about it?

The Home Secretary. I am grateful to my Right Hon. Friend for raising the matter. I am of course well aware of this concern, which I share. As a result I am able to announce a new Home Office initiative to be implemented under my personal supervision. A group of 40 Specially Trained Rapists, who are male, and 40 Specially Trained Rapees, who are female, has already been formed. They are known respectively as STRS and STRES. I am confident that with an active recruitment policy the number in each category will reach a target of 300 within the next 12 months. The purpose of the training is to enable the STRES to make and sustain allegations of rape against specific STRS who in turn are being trained as to the necessary ingredients of rape and in particular as to the best way of making admissions at their trial so as to ensure that they are convicted. They will then be sentenced to substantial terms of imprisonment. In this way, the public will be reassured as to the increased proportion of rapists who are convicted and generally in relation to the administration of the criminal justice system. This Hon. House will I know be pleased to learn that in no single instance will it be necessary for an actual rape to have taken place. In order to maintain a continuous supply of STRS and STRES, however, arrangements will be made for the various convictions to be quashed approximately one year after the sentence is imposed. This will reduce any possible criticism that the STRS`s Human Rights have been infringed and will have the further beneficial consequence of reducing serious overcrowding in our prisons which, I can assure Hon. Members of this House, will continue so long as I remain Home Secretary. In order to maintain public confidence, it will not be Home Office policy to publish statistics as to the number of convictions so quashed. In view of the unusual and stressful nature of their work, the STRS, and to a lesser extent the STRES, must be properly compensated. I am at present in consultation with my Right Hon. Friend the Chancellor of the Exchequer (*the Chancellor of the Exchequer nods*) both as to the appropriate level of remuneration and as to the possibility of an index-linked pension for these dedicated personnel. I am advised that for reasons of National security any such payments need to be made out of a specific but unidentified fund. I hope I have said sufficient to make it clear that yet again this Government is tackling a serious problem with imagination and determination. (Cries of "Hear, hear" and "Shame.")

The Shadow Home Secretary. Have the judges been consulted about this extraordinary scheme?

The Home Secretary. No indeed. I believe that, as with so many Home Office initiatives, the judges will oppose the plan and that therefore any form of consultation before it is up and running would simply be counterproductive. I am sure that Hon. Members of this House will agree that we alone know what is best for the electorate and that there is no place for judicial interference with carefully thought-out and imaginative proposals of Her Majesty`s Government. (Renewed cries of "Hear, hear" and "Shame.")

A loud female voice from the public gallery. As a woman who has been repeatedly raped, why don`t you bastards realise that the scheme is a load of diabolical crap?

The Deputy Speaker. Order! Order! Remove that woman. The dignity of the House is at stake. We must move on. The Hon. Member for Much Chipping has an important question about the prevalence of dry rot in his local vicarage.

CHRISTMAS NEWSLETTER

Hi everybody! You`re in luck! Here`s the annual report you`ve been waiting for from George and Anthea.

Well, we`ve had an exciting year!

In January, the weather was so poor that we decided to brighten things up by giving a party. We invited all our neighbours. Not all of them were able to come but those that did seemed to enjoy themselves. We provided lots of sausage-rolls and crisps and things and huge amounts of beer and wine which we got in a job-lot from our local supermarket. Some people were quite tipsy afterwards!

Nothing much happened in February or March but at Easter we took a deep breath and decided to go abroad because our usual haunt Skegness is sadly losing some of its charm. Amazingly, we hadn`t left these shores since our honeymoon in Majorca twenty-eight years ago. Some of you may remember that our honeymoon was not altogether successful because of the food and stomach-upsets and other things. Anyway, this time we did really well. We decided to take the Mini to France. We got it serviced - very necessary! - and made sure the insurance was all right. Then the great day came. We set off and went by the Channel

Tunnel. We both felt a bit seasick as we went through it but otherwise it was fine. At the far end, there were a few mishaps with other cars which appeared to be driving on the wrong side of the road but of course that`s what French people do. Anyway, George got the hang of it within a day or two. We stayed at a nice little hotel just outside Calais. We tried speaking to the owners in French because we had learnt the language at school - don`t ask how long ago that was! - but they didn`t seem to understand very well. We think they were probably a bit stupid. One day we went into a bistro and actually ate some snails. They were very good though an English couple at the next table said that we shouldn`t have eaten the shells. But then it turned out that they were paying their first ever visit abroad and so obviously didn`t know the ropes. We felt quite superior!

We haven`t told you how the children - no longer children of course! - are getting on. Well, David is still doing brilliantly as a loss-adjuster in Barrow-in-Furness. It`s handy for his main hobby which you will remember is fishing. Last week he caught a fish of some sort and cooked it himself and said it was delicious! Melanie is now sharing a flat with her friend Mandy in the Kings Cross area. They both work together in the same business which Mel says is part of the service industry. We suppose this is why they have to work such odd hours. It`s a bit strange and we don`t quite know what it involves but she always seems to have lots of cash so we think she must be pretty good at it!

In May it was of course George's birthday so we decided as a special treat to go to our local repertory theatre which as you know has got a high reputation. The production was a musical version of Hamlet. The cast was surprisingly small - only four in fact - and the music was pre-recorded but it was really quite good. For days afterwards, George walked round the house whistling "To be or not to be". Very funny.

This thespian experience spurred us on to immerse ourselves in even more culture. After much consultation we embarked upon a new enterprise, viz. reading the whole of the Encyclopaedia Brittanica. We enjoyed the first two volumes and now regard ourselves as well-equipped to take part in a Mastermind quiz so long as we can stick just to them! But we confess to struggling with the later volumes. We may return to them if we find time.

For our Summer hols we stayed as usual with Alan and Pam in their time-share near Wigan. It's a really nice apartment even though it is a bit cramped and rather hemmed in by other tower blocks. The countryside nearby is quite attractive away from the main roads and we spent lots of time walking during the day. Then back to the apartment for microwave meals followed by card games. Bliss! The only problem was that on the third day Anthea tripped and sprained her ankle but fortunately she was fine by the next day.

Then tragedy struck when we got home. We discovered that Sammy our favourite goldfish had died or "been called to Higher Service" as Anthea likes to describe it. A dreadful blow. We are still trying to come to terms with our loss. Edith suggested we should get a replacement but the truth is we can`t envisage another goldfish ever replacing our beloved Sammy.

Somehow the Summer just disappeared. In the Autumn we decided to go on a strict diet for a month. We needn`t explain the reasons! We spent ages browsing through the Readers` Digest which we get every month and eventually hit upon the watercress and dark-chocolate diet. Nobody - not even the experts - seems to know why it works but numerous readers testified to the fact that it really does. Our own experiences were rather mixed. Anthea certainly lost weight but often felt sick and dizzy. George surprisingly put on three pounds but in fairness was reasonably well most of the time and, as he explained to everyone, it did wonders for his piles.

After the leaves had fallen from the trees, we had heavy rain for a time. One of our drains got blocked and we had to get a man in to deal with it.

To end the year, we thought it would be exciting to enrol in some local classes. George put his name down for a course in the origins of plant life and Anthea did the same for advanced microwave cooking. Unhappily, both courses were full and we are still on the waiting-list. Better luck next time!

We are going to have our traditional Christmas with Bob and Sue and then, on New Year`s Eve, we will as always bring in the New Year with Rod and Lynn whilst watching an old video. Our new year resolution is to cut down on drink so we intend to greet the new year with a glass of cranberry juice.

So, Season`s Greetings! Here`s hoping we all have another fantastic year!

TAKING THE OATH

(An extract from the author's play, *Are You Courting?*)

Monday morning.

Kate (*a pupil, to Sebastian her barrister pupil master*). So what are you doing today? Are you courting? (*This is said in a way that suggests the joke is far from new.*)

Sebastian. Yes, I've a personal injury case, liability now admitted so just damages. And later, a conference with Lucy. She's a solicitor friend of mine. Oddly enough she used to be a vet. Then one day she had a revelation and saw the Light.

Kate. On the road to Damascus?

Sebastian. No, actually. In the saloon-bar of a ferry-boat coming back from the Isle of Wight. Some noisy passengers were arguing as to which one had the most incompetent solicitor and she thought, "What a challenge!" But there *are* times now when she seems to think that life was a lot easier when all she had to do was to shove one arm up a cow's arse.

Kate. Vets must do other things besides that! But how did you meet her?

Sebastian. She came along to court when her firm instructed me to defend a man charged with causing grievous bodily harm. Our client had carefully carried a large pan of boiling oil from his kitchen. Then he flung it out of an upstairs window onto a door-to-door salesman standing below.

Kate. What was the defence?

Sebastian. Accident. That didn`t work. Our client got five years. So we crawled off to a wine-bar to drown our sorrows, and after a few glasses the strictly professional relationship between us, well, it went for a burton.

Kate. So what`s the personal injury case about?

Sebastian (skimming through his brief). I am for the Claimant. A plumber from Peckham. Lost his left big toe in a road accident. Ruined his life apparently. Has had to give up his main hobby of *Morris* dancing. And he can`t even play football with his children.

Kate. How old are they?

Sebastian Kylie is five, Britney is four and Madonna is two. There`s another on the way of course but because of his missing toe he and his wife almost gave up sex for a time.

Kate. Almost? For how long?

Sebastian. Nearly ten days.

Kate. I don`t want to appear critical but aren`t you on a bum case?

Sebastian. Certainly not! The man has lost his job and there's a large claim for loss of earnings. The trouble is: the other side have offered sixty thousand, so unless we beat that we're up the creek. And I happen to know that there's not much chance of a settlement because the Defendant's insurers have got a particularly difficult claims manager. Apparently, this man has an ulcer which gives him a stab of pain every time he has to fork out money for his company.

Kate. Great! Can I come along for the entertainment?

<u>Later in court.</u>

Sebastian. I call the Claimant to give evidence about the effect which the accident has had on him.

The Claimant limps uneasily towards the witness-box. The usher is ready for him.

Usher. What's your religion?

Claimant. I am redundant.

Usher (to judge). I think he's an agnostic.

Judge. Very well. Let him affirm.

Claimant. Can't I swear on the Bible?

Usher. No, not unless you've got religious beliefs.

Claimant. But I *have* got religious beliefs.

Usher. No, you can't have, not if you're an agnostic.

Judge. Far be it for me to interrupt this theological debate but we really must get on. Usher, give the Book to the

Claimant. I want him to look inside the front cover. I will then ask him whether it is the appropriate Testament.

Book handed to Claimant who opens the front cover.

Judge. What does it say?

Claimant (slowly). It says, "This is the property of the Department for Constitutional Affairs". Is that one of them new religious sects?

(*Laughter in court, particularly from the Defendant`s camp.*)

Judge (indulgently). The correct title these days is "The Ministry of Justice", but I doubt whether it`s one of those Ministries that can be called a religious sect.

(*As it is a joke made by the judge, everyone falls about.*)

Sebastian (in a whisper to his solicitor). No one will take our client seriously now. It`s a bad start.

Solicitor (gloomily). Let`s hope it`s not the finish.

Printed in the United Kingdom
by Lightning Source UK Ltd.
123916UK00003B/79-81/A